COUNTRY LIVING

Stylish Makeovers

Design Ideas for Every Room

Text by Rhoda Murphy
Foreword by Nancy Mernit Soriano

Hearst Books
A Division of Sterling Publishing Co., Inc.
New York

For Country Living
Editor-in-Chief Nancy Mernit Soriano
Art Director Susan M. Netzel
Deputy Editor Lawrence A. Bilotti

Produced by Smallwood & Stewart, Inc.
New York City
Book Design Amy Henderson
Appendix Text Laura Tringale

Jacket photography all by Keith Scott Morton except spine photo by David Prince

Rhoda Murphy would like to thank the following people for their help with this project: Dave Ackerman of Architectural Salvage, Linda Banks of Banks Interior Design Associates, Nick Bensley of Nick Bensley Architects, Shirley and George Bianco, Amy Butler, Arlene and Gregory Chiaramonte, Brian Cooper of Early New England Restorations, Clark Frankel, Les Fossel of Restoration Resources, Randy Florke, Jeff Harris of Vintage Log & Lumber, Ramona Hughes, Keith Keegan, Jessica Levine, Ken Muth of Wood Natural Restorations, Joan and Sid Osofsky of Hammertown Barn, Mary and Bill Radke, Jeff Steele and Bob McKinnon, Sheri and Jim Swinehart, Peri Wolfman, and her husband, Mike Murphy.

Library of Congress Cataloging-in-Publication Data Available.

10 9 8 7 6 5 4 3 2 1

First Paperback Edition 2004
Published by Hearst Books
A Division of Sterling Publishing Co., Inc.
387 Park Avenue South, New York, NY 10016

Country Living is a trademark owned by Hearst Magazines Property, Inc., in USA, and Hearst Communications, Inc., in Canada. Hearst Books is a trademark owned by Hearst Communications, Inc.

www.countryliving.com

Distributed in Canada by
Sterling Publishing
C/o Canadian Manda Group, One Atlantic Avenue, Suite 105
Toronto, Ontario, Canada M6K 3E7

Distributed in Australia by Capricorn Link (Australia) Pty. Ltd.
P.O. Box 704, Windsor, NSW 2756
Australia

Printed in China

ISBN 1-58816-402-0

Foreword

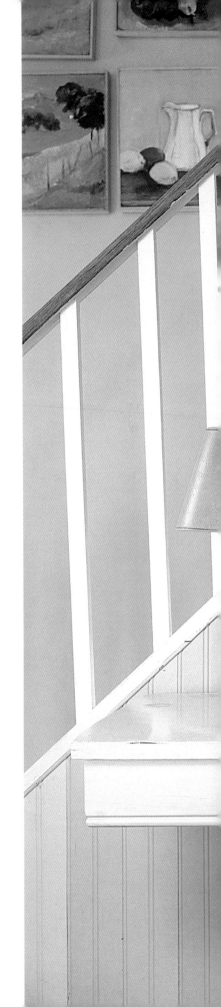

For most of us, our homes are works in progress: places we build or rebuild, rearrange or reorganize, modify or redecorate, as our lives evolve. The desire for all this change often arises out of necessity, like remodeling a kitchen to make it more functional, or out of pleasure, like testing a new paint color. Whether you're living through a renovation or fantasizing about it, there's something fascinating about the process of turning dreams and drawings into reality.

Every year at *Country Living* magazine we get to see dozens of such dreams realized. They range in size from simple decorating projects to complete kitchen makeovers to total restorations from the floorboards up. Each project follows a slightly different path, but all have the same goal in mind: to introduce new updates and modern conveniences while preserving the charm and patina of the original. On the following pages are some of our favorite renovations, together with useful tips gathered over the years. If you're thinking of a change for your home, we hope this book will provide all the necessary inspiration, advice, and encouragement to make a stylish renovation a dream come true.

Nancy Mernit Soriano

EDITOR-IN-CHIEF
Country Living

Introduction

THERE ARE THREE KINDS OF PEOPLE who love old houses. First, there are the

purists, who want to step into the past the minute the door is opened. They search for

craftsmen to hew beams by hand, to trowel on genuine horsehair plaster instead of

drywall. They research appropriate fabrics and paint colors and furnish the entire

house in period. As an owner in Ohio puts the

purist philosophy, "If you are a custodian of a

period house . . . you owe it to the house to do

what is appropriate for it. You really don't own

the house. It is entrusted to you." And therein

lies the purist's greatest quandary: how to make

an old house compatible with a contemporary lifestyle while remaining true to the structure. | Next come the pragmatists. Although they still love their homes, they don't eschew modern materials or methods. They will restore an old window or door, for example, but not if a better or more efficient substitute can be found. Updating an old house to reflect current taste and conveniences is a venerable practice that

is hotly debated among old-house aficionados—and one that has sometimes been taken too far. Victorian building books gave instructions on how to "update" Greek Revival houses with turrets, gingerbread, and porches. In the mid-20th century, those same Victorian buildings were

stripped of their decorative elements in an effort to make them appear more "modern." Now we tend to appreciate architectural periods for their own distinct characteristics and don't try to make a house look like a different animal altogether. | Finally, there are the revisionists, those who love classic architecture but would rather live in a new structure. They construct houses in a classic style, lavish them with traditional details—deep wood moldings or old-fashioned hardware, for example—and furnish them with old farm tables or cupboards. In many ways, they have the best of both worlds and can

freely alter the historical to fit a contemporary way

of life. | What makes an old house so appealing to

all of these people? First, old houses were built indi-

vidually and largely by hand. That doesn't mean they're necessarily better—although

craftsmanship was often finer than today—but the builder's skills did imbue the

finished structure with a distinctive character. Second, some elements were simply

better in the past. Old-growth wood was denser and stronger, floorboards wider,

moldings more intricate, windows handmade. Finally, the patina that comes only with

age adds an irresistible quality that is part romance, part history. In a house, the

imprint of time—the worn floorboards or fading paint—adds a layer of personality that reminds us—in the best possible way—that houses are living places that evolve

and change. | The renovation projects in this book celebrate not so much old

houses themselves but the values we find so appealing in them—the sense of quality,

attention to detail, and character. In these pages you'll find examples of all three

approaches to renovation, and you'll learn how to blend a new addition into an old

house or infuse a new home with personality. You'll find

suggestions for improving the exterior of your house and

for rendering your living room, kitchen, and bathroom

livable and stylish while still retaining all the characteris-

tics that made you fall in love with them in the first place.

Living Areas

MORE THAN OTHER ROOMS in the house, living areas can be seen as barometers of social fashion and the way we live. In bygone eras, these rooms were lavished with details: thick walls, gracious fireplaces, wide floorboards, elaborate woodwork and moldings. Kitchens and less public areas were finished and decorated quite modestly by comparison. Guests were ushered into a formal front parlor and would rarely see any other part of the house; some earlier homes even had two entrances—one for visitors and one for family and the help. | Today, the way we use our living spaces has changed. We generally prefer more spacious rooms to a multitude of small ones. We like rooms that flow easily into one another as opposed to the discrete public/private spaces of the past. We enjoy living

areas that are much more relaxed and versatile, and that are able to play the role of both family room and formal room. Architecturally, this means that living areas are opening up to other rooms in the house, especially the kitchen. Decoratively, this means that furnishings in living areas are becoming more informal and idiosyncratic. | *Juggling old and new can be tricky but several successful and inspiring approaches are featured on the following pages. One of the homeowners chose to leave the original house intact and put a living room addition*

on the back. Another family loved old log houses,

but didn't wish to live in a 600-square-foot house,

so they combined several aging log structures to create a single home with many living

areas. Their converted barn features soaring ceilings and wide-open rooms and affords the

freedom to put walls, windows, and doors almost anywhere without the constraints

imposed by an existing structure. And though it's no easy

task to construct a new building and give it the qualities

of a classic house, one homeowner did just that by adding

salvaged mantels, reclaimed floors and trim, and rescued

hardware and doors to his contemporary house.

A Passion for Details

As the owner of this 1787 Connecticut Cape will attest, restoration takes time, money, and above all a certain obsessive attention to detail. He spent eight painstaking years making his home appear as it might have when it was built just after the American Revolution. (A little of the house's history was revealed when workmen opened up a wall and found a bill, dated 1802, for Captain Timothy Shailer.) The idea of restoring it using only old wood and a minimum of machine-made materials came upon him slowly. "I lived in it for three years before I realized what I had," the homeowner recalls. "Then I was driven to bring it back to what it was."

Wherever possible he used antique materials—most of the hardware, for instance, is early-19th-century—but if those were unavailable, he employed experts who crafted surfaces using 18th-century methods. Modern amenities were deftly disguised: Switchplates, for instance, were camouflaged in hand-hammered sconces; wires were hidden behind panels or inside beams. His kitchen sink was carved out of a massive chunk of rough granite. "When the whole thing was done," he says, "you felt as if you were back in an earlier time. That was the kind of magic I was looking for."

Luckily, the footprint of this Connecticut house had remained unchanged through the years. Using a contractor who specializes in restoration, the homeowner eliminated all modern notes. Previous owners had left many original elements untouched, including the stone wall (the fence was added), the chimney, and a few glass panes. For verisimilitude, craftsmen hand-made every shake on the new roof. No traces of old paint could be found, so the homeowner painted the exterior a brownish-red hue, a common shade of the period.

Restoration was still in progress when these photographs were taken. The false beams and new plasterboard were later eliminated in the keeping room (ABOVE), located just off the kitchen. All the furniture is of the period, including the slip-covered settee and early-18th-century hutch as well as the painted cupboard. To achieve an 18th-century look in the parlor (RIGHT), the owner removed the plaster ceiling to expose the chestnut floorboards above it and replaced missing beams with antique timbers. After he pulled off the wallpaper, he loved the ravaged look of the walls so much that he left them. Some time later, he had a plasterer strip the walls down to the old lath and replaster them in genuine horsehair plaster. The pointer doorstop is one of the owner's few 20th-century indulgences.

Preserving Old Plaster Walls

Until the end of the 19th century, most walls were covered in lime plaster—a mixture of either ground limestone or oyster shells, sand, and fiber from hog or cattle hair (although called horsehair plaster, the hair rarely came from horses). Lime plaster was applied in a labor-intensive three-coat process and had to dry for up to a year before it was ready for papering or painting. Around 1900, gypsum was introduced. It was more affordable, set faster (in two to three weeks), was harder, and looked virtually identical to lime plaster.

The lime plaster process is so expensive that most restorationists use gypsum plaster or a new alternative called veneer plaster (a two-coat process where plaster is applied over gypsum-core panels, commonly known as "bluewall"). The process captures the softness and texture of old plaster at only a slightly greater cost than regular drywall.

KEEP MOISTURE OUT

Treated well, plaster will last almost forever. Its biggest enemy is moisture, which causes it to disintegrate. Outside, check roofs, gutters, and downspouts frequently to make sure no water is seeping into the house. Watch for plumbing leaks inside. Efflorescence, a powdery substance on the surface of a wall, will betray the presence of moisture. Once the source of the dampness is detected and eliminated, the powdery deposits can simply be scrubbed away with a stiff brush.

BE NICE

If you have plaster walls, you can take some steps to help preserve them. Avoid drilling into plaster, if possible. Use proper picture nails when hanging pictures, never regular nails. Better still, install a picture rail and avoid making holes in the plaster altogether.

REPAIR CRACKS AND HOLES

Most old plaster walls have cracks. Hairline cracks can be sealed with a filling material. Close wider cracks with fiberglass mesh tape and cover with a skim of plaster.

CALL IN THE PROS

Plastering is tricky and generally not something the average weekender can tackle. Anything bigger than a small crack—such as sagging plaster, large holes, or bulges—requires professional help. Ceilings can be shored up by new techniques that involve injecting special adhesive into the plaster; larger holes may need three coats of plaster to build the area up to the original surface. Bulges in a wall may require removal of the plaster and restoration of the old lath.

EXPERIMENT WITH PAINT TECHNIQUES

If you crave the look of old plaster but lack the budget, you can achieve something of the effect through paint techniques. Experiment with color glazes or washes, following the instructions in a good book on decorative painting.

Hand-Hewn Comfort

To elicit the past rather than re-create it was the mission of the couple who built this home in central Mississippi. To that end, they united two antique log structures and adapted them to a plan for a new ten-room house that evokes the rugged character of a dwelling from the 19th century.

A circa-1850s two-story log house that the couple found in Kentucky forms the center section, which is made up of the foyer, dining room, and two upstairs bedrooms. Another building, a one-room 1860s Mississippi cabin that the pair dismantled themselves, numbering each timber, became their den (which gives an idea of how small many old structures are by today's standards). New wings containing the kitchen, sun porch, and master bedroom used the same squared-off logs to blend with the old portions of the house.

The hand-hewn poplar beams of an 1860s cabin form a rustic backdrop in the family's den (LEFT). Cypress lapped siding used on the exterior (RIGHT) makes the two cabins that together compose the house look as one.

New portions of the Mississippi house blend with the old thanks to judicious use of rescued materials—log walls, flooring, and paneling—culled from Southern buildings dating as far back as the mid-19th century. An early-1800s pine table from Tennessee claims center stage in the dining room in the 1850s section of the house. The antique table features a revolving central serving tray made of poplar anchored by a cypress lamp stand. An electrified reproduction chandelier hangs overhead. Other antiques, chosen for their original painted finishes, include a stack of pantry boxes, an 1830s Georgia hunt board, and a glazed yellow-pine step-back cupboard from the 1880s.

Living in a Log Cabin

Old log cabins are the very embodiment of our pioneer past; many date back to the late 1600s in the mid-Atlantic region and their popularity peaked in the frontier expansion between 1750 and 1850. Although the logs were always held in place by their own weight, various styles of corner notching were used, and the logs could be square or round. Typically, joints between the logs were chinked with mud plaster or covered with rough wood siding. Spruce and pine were the preferred woods.

Few log homes survive from the 18th and 19th centuries because they were often abandoned in favor of larger structures. Those that do survive are small by today's standards, ranging in size from just 600 to 1,200 square feet. To make them practical for modern living, two or more cabins are often combined, with an effort to keep as much of the original structures—especially the window openings—intact.

LOG ENEMIES

After termites, powder post beetles, and carpenter ants (get regular inspections for insect activity), water is the greatest enemy of log cabins. In fact, logs need very little upkeep as long as they aren't exposed to long-term moisture and are able to dry out properly. A good roof with a deep soffit is critical to protect the logs from rain and snow.

MATCH THEM UP

Early log cabins were one-room structures, but they quickly evolved into a series of two or three connected rectangular rooms. If you plan to combine buildings, consult with an expert first. If the logs have been cut in the same way and the notching on the wood is the same, your costs should be lower.

CHINKING MATTERS

The solid material, or chinking, that fills the gaps between the timber is as important as the logs. In the old days, mud mixed with straw or cattle hair formed the chinking; now masons apply special concrete to the chinks both inside and outside the house. Usually, the chinking material is tinted to harmonize with the color of the lumber. A good chinking job can last up to a hundred years. If the chinking is crumbly or has holes, it is possible that moisture has seeped in and that individual logs may be damaged and will have to be replaced.

An Old Barn
Gains New Life

Sitting abandoned and forgotten in a Vermont field on Lake Champlain, the 1790s barn was one step away from caving in when it was rescued by a barn relocation company. They carefully took down the post-and-beam construction and put up a modified version in Long Island, New York, transforming it from a place for animals and hay into a warm and spacious family home. In the process they retained the barn's best qualities—soaring ceilings, ancient paneling, thick visible beams—and combined them with the attributes of a house—separate rooms and plenty of windows. To blend the structure in with its suburban surroundings, they clad the exterior in cedar shingles and painted the trim white.

A pair of new wings constructed from recycled building materials—weathered wood beams, old barn siding, and vintage doors—echoes the look of the main house. One wing houses the kitchen and family room; the other contains the master suite and two bedrooms.

This 18th-century barn lives on in the form of a generously proportioned house (LEFT). The original barn doors and a high transom window hint at the building's barn ancestry.

Inside the front entrance (OPPOSITE), sunlight floods into the great room via door sidelights, a transom window, and a window above. The architects retained the barn's dramatic 26-foot-high ceilings and massive hand-hewn exposed beams. Large two-foot-square slate tiles form the new floor.

A trio of vintage window frames (ABOVE) installed in the master suite landing provides a vantage point for observing the great room (RIGHT), which is a part of the original barn. Such strong architecture demands hefty furnishings (anything dainty would get lost in such a space). Generously proportioned upholstered pieces hold their own and bring an air of comfort to the room. Paneled wooden shutters on the lower windows serve as an alternative to curtains and allow the architecture to show. High windows are left unadorned. Built of vintage oak beams faced with limestone, the new fireplace blends unobtrusively with the barn framing.

Making a
Barn a Home

Not so long ago, barns dotted the American landscape. But as agrarian life disappears, so do the buildings that were essential to it. Many barns represented the very best crafts-manship of their time, work that will never be seen again. Rather than leaving aging barns to deteriorate, experts can transform them into homes. Several companies specialize in finding old barns, taking them apart, and rebuilding them in a new setting—it's a way to create a home as well as preserve a valuable piece of history.

ENVELOP THE OUTSIDE WALLS

Barns were never meant to retain heat, so insulation is a priority. Today this can be very effectively done through a system of foam panels that encircle the exterior of the structure like a blanket. These panels can be covered with salvaged siding or clapboards. Window openings are precut to the architect's specifications at the factory. Inside, the original siding can remain exposed.

CHOOSE YOUR SHAPE WELL

Because most barns are post-and-beam structures, they can be shortened relatively easily, but the width is very difficult to change. For that reason, it's best to stick with the existing measurements of the barn. In addition, the placement of interior walls is dictated by the location of the horizontal supports. Partitions can be placed only at the beam points, not between the beams.

PLAY WITH THE WINDOWS

Unlike an old house, where an owner feels obliged to keep the existing fenestration, a barn is almost a blank canvas. Indeed, barns would be gloomy places unless windows were added. This lack of historical precedent gives a homeowner wonderful freedom to add windows of almost any shape or size, wherever they look best.

Early American
Beauty

For a pair of self-described antiquarians, living in a Revolutionary War-era house was a dream come true. For years, the Cincinnati couple had been collecting 17th- and early-18th-century American antiques, but did not have a home suitable to display their furnishings. That is, not until the 1778 hip-roofed home came on the market. It was love at first sight. The house is certainly an oddity in Ohio. An import from the East, it is at least a decade older than any other structure here. In 1953, a fellow old-house aficionado moved the dwelling (it was slated to be torn down for a new post office) from Watertown, Connecticut, to Cincinnati. "In the vernacular, it was what we call a 'virgin house'", says one of the present owners. "Lack of money is often the best preserver of buildings, and this one was virtually untouched." The wide floorboards, the stairs, the paneling in the dining room—all were as they had been 200 years earlier. To preserve the period character, the previous owners had consulted Colonial Williamsburg experts about paint colors. Although the wall hues do not reflect current findings about Colonial paint, which reveal them to have been much more brilliant than thought, the current homeowners enjoy the colors so much they have left them unchanged.

In the front entry, the reddish-brown doors and robin's-egg-blue trim have remained the same since the 1950s. The walnut tall-case clock dates to the late 1770s and is but one in the homeowners' collection of 17 examples. The double doors and bull's-eye windowpanes are original to the house, as are the floors and stairway. The stairs are the only part of the house that was transported from Connecticut intact; everything else was broken down and moved in numbered pieces.

Although the dining
room is electrified, there are
no lamps or electric fixtures
in the room. The couple
prefers to illuminate it with
an early-19th-century
16-candle Scandinavian
chandelier. Other period
furnishings include a 1760s
drop-leaf mahogany table
from New York, Chippendale
chairs of the same era from
Delaware, and an 1810
Tennessee walnut hunt board.
The Pennsylvania corner
cupboard has its original
paint; it houses blue-and-
white Chinese export
porcelain. A hand-painted
floorcloth adorns the

Historic Colors
and Finishes

Although for years it was believed that paint hues from the Colonial period were muted, the colors were actually quite brilliant; early paint research failed to take into account the fact that color changes occur over time.

LOOK TO THE EXPERTS

To determine precisely what color your old house or your walls once were, hire a historical paint consultant. These experts use stereomicroscopes and other high-tech tools to determine early paint colors used in your house. To find one, look on the Internet, call your local historical society, or consult the Landmark yellow pages published by the National Trust for Historic Preservation. (See **Resources**, page 182.) The consultant will take into consideration chemical changes in the paint and will tell you what the colors looked like at the time they were painted.

If you simply want paint colors that are appropriate for your house, there are several books that can give you suggestions. Or, work with paint consultants who can use photographs of your house to give you a range of suitable colors. If it's a very old house, keep in mind that the earliest paint tints were earth pigments that yielded ochre, red, umber, and green. Uncommon colors such as Prussian blue came from rarer minerals and hence were more costly.

COLOR THE WOODWORK

Up until the early-20th century, white woodwork was uncommon. Walls were usually lighter than the trim (the reverse of what is commonly done today) and the moldings often featured decorative paint treatments that mimicked fine wood graining. To modern eyes, this deep brown shellacked trim of yesteryear seems to suck the light out of rooms, and the thick coats of lacquer hide fine detailing. However, painting over it can be difficult. Usually, the trim needs to be sanded down before it can be repainted. For a crisp, clean look, paint the woodwork a glossy bright white and the walls a strong color. Or try the alternative and paint the trim in a bold hue—vivid green or strong blue, for example, and contrast it with white walls. Depending on the age and style of your house, you may want to consider hiring a decorative painter to make your trim mimic marble, grained wood, such as mahogany or tiger maple, or even tortoiseshell.

Stenciling and Painted Finishes

For most people in Colonial America, wall-paper was an unaffordable luxury. Like their counterparts in Sweden and Germany, some Colonists turned to stenciling. Stencils provided an inexpensive way to brighten a home and express creativity.

Stenciling—and other decorative finishes—can do more than just beautify a room or add a period feeling. They can underscore a room's good points and help camouflage the bad ones. For instance, a stencil around the inside edge of a too-low ceiling will lend it visual height. Conversely, if a ceiling is very high, a stencil painted around the top and again at the bottom of the wall will "shrink" it, and make the room feel more intimate. In rooms bereft of decorative moldings, painted designs— even columns—can be inexpensively and stunningly created.

FIND STENCIL INSPIRATION

Traditional stencil designs are readily available at craft shops or through Internet sources. But making your own patterns is easy. Because stencils are usually very simple shapes such as stylized fruit or flowers that gain effect through repetition, even non-artists can draw them. Look for inspiration in wall-paper books, tile patterns, and fabrics.

STENCIL A BORDER

Stencils can be applied to virtually any surface with almost any kind of paint.

▓ For best results, make sure that your stenciling paint is thicker than usual by allowing it to sit uncovered for a few minutes before you start painting. This improves your control over the paint and reduces the likelihood of smudges.

▓ The best tool for stenciling is a stencil brush or your index finger wrapped in a square of velour fabric.

▓ Apply the paint to the stencil with a pouncing motion, working from the edges of the cutout to the center.

▓ Keep the stencil flat against the surface and frequently wipe the edges clean with a cloth.

CREATE A VENERABLE AURA

Paint techniques on walls are yet another method of bringing personality and interest to a room. There are many books that explain, step-by-step, how to accomplish easy decorative paint methods. Walls can be artificially aged with paint (using nothing more than paint and furniture paste wax, which is applied in places to keep the paint from adhering; the paint is then rubbed off randomly); glazed; rag-rolled; or sponged. All bring subtle pattern and intriguing colors to a space.

If you are stenciling new walls, create the illusion of being faded over time: Apply stencils with an almost dry brush, use muted colors that have been thinned with glazing liquid, or cover completed stencils with a tinted glaze.

A Family Farmhouse

Adding on to a venerable structure is never easy. The new part must meld with the old, yet still solve the problems that necessitated its being built in the first place. A couple with a late-18th-century farmhouse in upstate New York faced just this dilemma. They loved their house, but it was too small. They needed a sunny multipurpose great room where they could entertain their large extended family. In deciding to add on such a space, the couple committed themselves to maintaining the historic character of the house. To achieve this, the pair placed the addition at the back of the house so that it would not interrupt the elegant facade. Inside, they incorporated salvaged wood and paneling into the room's construction, paved the floor in old bluestone from New England, and installed a late-18th-century mantel.

Once a stagecoach stop on the Old Post Road, the six-bedroom farmhouse in upstate New York (LEFT) boasts 13 fireplaces and five chimneys. The large fireplace in the new great room (RIGHT), which juts out from the back of the house, ensures that the space remains warm and inviting, and a wall of French doors fills the room with sunlight.

Despite the new addition, the family still loves the old farmhouse's original sitting room, where they lounge in front of the fire on the deep, extra-long daybed. A historic salmon hue emphasizes the deep window wells. Upholstery and furnishings are kept casual so that people feel relaxed. A vintage Oriental rug covers the original wood floors.

Salvaging Old Mantels

Although it has long since lost its practical role as an important source of heat, the fireplace is still a spiritual focus for a room. Sadly, many fine mantels were torn out and chimneys bricked up with the advent of central heating—stripping rooms of a great deal of personality. But this does mean that there is a large stock of salvaged mantels, from the very simple to the elaborately carved, readily available from antiques stores and dealers in architectural artifacts. In fact, an old mantel can sometimes cost less than having a new one made. If a room has lost its fireplace, consider re-installing a mantel, even if getting the chimney working again is impractical. It will add greatly to the character of the space.

MEASURE THE OPENING

If you plan on using your fireplace, there must be at least six inches of clearance from the fireplace opening to the edge of the mantel. Be sure to check with your local building department about codes that govern the placement of mantels.

LOOK AT CONDITION

Salvaged mantels are readily available from architectural antiques dealers and even flea markets. Although a salvaged piece may be cheaper than a new one, don't forget to factor in the cost of installation, especially if the old mantel is in pieces. When buying a salvaged mantel, make sure that all the pieces are intact and in good condition, especially if the mantel is metal or stone. Take lots of measurements and check with your architect, contractor, or carpenter on installation issues. If you are considering installing a heavy stone or cast-iron mantel, for example, your hearth may need structural support.

KEEP TO SCALE

Choose a mantel appropriate to your house and the room. If you have a Colonial home, an ornate Victorian mantel will look out of place. Consider scale: For example, some mantels were designed for bedrooms and smaller rooms and would look inappropriate in a large dining room. By the same token, don't buy a mantel that's too big. If the piece is too large, it will look awkward and out of proportion.

The Age of
Elegance, Reborn

Beneath the 1960s red shag carpeting, the thin-strip oak floor, the makeshift wall dividers, and countless coats of paint lay a lovely Federal-style house in Long Island, New York, waiting to be rediscovered. It was this knowledge that sustained the owners as they embarked on what was to be a year-long renovation (they did much of the work themselves). In many ways the modern touches had preserved the house: Beneath the cheap flooring and worn carpeting lay original wide-plank wood floors in almost perfect condition. The makeshift panels that had divided the structure into a two-family dwelling had protected the period detailing and trim; a blanket of paint covered lead medallions that adorned the outside of the windows. With the abundant Federal detail revealed, the owners realized that relatively little was required to make the interior come to life again.

Elegant architectural features abound in the 1832 residence (LEFT). A plywood panel had been nailed into the archway of the front hall (OPPOSITE) when the house was converted into a two-family dwelling. When the panel was removed, the arch proved to be in almost perfect condition. Painstaking scraping of multiple paint layers revealed the incredible details of the trim. At first, the owners hesitated to paint the original floor in the entrance hall, but they wanted to define the area. As they had left the floors virtually untouched elsewhere in the house, they decided to go ahead and paint.

Interior Trim

Just as accessories complement a lovely dress, so does decorative trim imbue a home with elegance. Originally, millwork—the 18th-century word for work from the sawmill—served a purpose: Crown and baseboard moldings hid the gaps where the walls met the ceiling or floor; chair rails protected the plaster from chair backs; picture rails enabled homeowners to hang artwork without damaging the walls. Over time, these wooden accents grew more elaborate.

When selecting trim, suitability is key. The moldings must be in keeping with the style of the house and in proportion to the room. For instance, a wide crown molding on a room with a low ceiling will make it appear top-heavy. But a lavish baseboard can create the illusion of height. With the addition of the right trim, plain windows or doorways can be given a distinctive visual presence.

DON'T FORGET LABOR

Rather than springing for a costly single piece of molding with an intricate profile (the contours of the woodwork), a cost-cutting technique is to cluster several small trims. Remember, however, that each piece of molding needs to be applied separately. So, if you are grouping three pieces of trim, your labor costs will be triple what they would be if you were applying a single piece.

MATCH YOUR WOODWORK

If you are putting on an addition or restoring decorative woodwork in an existing room, you may have difficulty finding an exact match for your trim. If you don't mind the expense, one option is to have the woodwork reproduced by a mill that specializes in custom work. Or—a more economical solution—you can simply opt to choose moldings that are similar—not identical—to trim in neighboring rooms.

ADD MOLDINGS TO WALLS

To dress up a room, create the look of paneling by applying moldings to the wall. Tape out squares and rectangles on the wall and attach the trim. To highlight the details, paint them a contrasting shade from the walls.

KNOW YOUR STUFF

The least expensive solid-wood molding is made of paint-grade pine. It includes what's known as "finger-jointed" pieces, which are assembled from shorter segments. Next is regular pine and then poplar. Poplar is a sound choice—it cuts easily, shrinks minimally, and takes paint well. If you splurge on hardwoods such as cherry, maple, and oak, keep in mind that labor will cost more as well: Nail holes must be predrilled. Such hardwood trims should be stained instead of painted to show off their color and grain. An alternative is medium-density fiberboard, which is made of wood fiber and is cheaper than paint-grade pine. It is also less likely than solid wood to split or warp.

A Loving Rescue and Revival

Almost every beautiful old house—after mistreatment or neglect—needs a fairy godparent who can wave a magic wand and make the house lovely again. Thirty years ago, this 1805 dwelling near Rhinebeck, New York, was in need of just such a transformation. Once an elegant Greek Revival house, it had been left to fall apart and was virtually uninhabitable.

Fortunately, the house was bought by a man whose hobbies were a bit unusual for that time. He journeyed to junkyards and garage sales ferreting out old doors, period knobs, and old wood to replace pieces that had been removed or destroyed. He scraped layers of paint off the graceful woodwork. The owner also eliminated inappropriate additions and returned the structure

to its 19th-century roots. "He made it live again," says the present owner, an antiques dealer who bought the house from the restorer and now does his bit to keep this Cinderella looking her very best.

Thirty years ago, the gentleman who renovated this five-bedroom 1805 house (LEFT) purchased it from a descendant of the original settlers of this part of the Hudson River Valley. Doors at either end of the center hall were a common design feature of the time (OPPOSITE). They allowed for excellent cross ventilation. The present owner has filled the house with suitable antiques and fabrics. A deacon's bench from Rhode Island rests on the original floors. Two family dogs pose on a handwoven stair runner in a classic American design.

The man who restored
the house was a practical
sort—he wanted to make the
home livable. To that end,
he extended the dining room.
All the floors here are new
but made from old wood.
The mantel is original. Today's
owners have decorated it
with their collection of
toleware trays that date from
the mid-19th century to the
1940s. For the walls, they
consulted a historical paint
palette and finally settled on
the soft Williamsburg green.
In this setting, reproductions
and antiques mix with ease.
A Georgian barrel-back pine
settee dates from around
1830, while the Windsor
chairs and the gateleg table
are reproductions.

Choosing Window Treatments

Old houses often have great architecture in abundance. To make the most of that asset, consider window treatments that reveal windows rather than cover them up. Modest treatments will also keep attention on wonderful antiques or a stunning fireplace.

SET PRIORITIES

Before you pick a window treatment, determine your needs. To bring just a bit of color and softness to windows, opt for simple swags such as those in the photograph opposite. These mount onto a wooden board that is attached to the top of the window frame. If privacy is important, select shades—such as the Roman shades shown at left—or curtains that block the view but still allow control of light and air. To soften the window lines and diffuse the light, choose a blissfully simple single panel like the one shown in the photograph above. This muslin panel is shirred onto a tension rod suspended within the window frame.

STAY TRUE TO YOUR HOME

Keep in mind the look and style of your home when deciding on window dressings. Luxurious, billowy curtains will look inappropriate in a farmhouse. Fine antiques call for equally graceful windows. Floor-length silk curtains or elaborate swags and jabots would be fitting in a Federal-style home, for instance. The type of fabric will determine the style of the window treatment. Gossamer thin sheers shirred on rods, or light cotton prints with tabs, suit a casual, country-style room.

LOOK AT SHUTTERS

For a clean, architectural appearance, consider installing shutters (or their handsome but less costly cousin, wood blinds) indoors. Solid wood shutters look elegant, but they are expensive. They block the light but offer nothing in terms of light or air control. Wide-slatted plantation shutters are slightly less costly, and their adjustable slats allow air and light to enter.

Light and Life
Fill an Old Mill

Two hundred years ago, this gristmill was an integral part of daily life in Pennsylvania's Bucks County. Residents brought their wheat here to be ground into flour. But until recently, plain wood siding added in the 1950s camouflaged the venerable structure. When the present owners saw the building, they envisioned a way to retain the spirit of the mill's past while making it thoroughly livable for the present.

First, off came the siding to reveal the original wood and stone exterior. Then the restorers turned to the interior. Previous owners had already converted the structure into a residence, and some elements of the past still remained—the original rock walls, chestnut beams, and wideboard pumpkin-pine floors. But it was dark and airless, as most mills tend to be. To open up the four-story building and bring plenty of light and air to its seven rooms, the architect combined three staircases into one, added new windows, and removed the living room ceiling.

The stream that once powered the gristmill still runs beneath the house (LEFT), filling it with the music of flowing water. New six-over-six windows and transoms flood the home with light and feature handmade glass that looks old. The new shutters recall traditional barn doors. A single new staircase (OPPOSITE) links the mill's four levels. The flight of stairs was constructed from remilled 200-year-old pine that was artificially aged with chains and ice picks. Hung so it can be raised and lowered on a pulley, a late-19th-century iron chandelier illuminates the stairway come nightfall.

A river runs through it: In the second-level living room, the new fireplace was crafted from stones gathered along a nearby creek. The mantel had a previous life as a beam in a now-razed barn. Because the mill is set in the woods, far from neighboring houses, no window-covering curtains or shades were necessary, so the rustic setting is visible in every room. Pennsylvania antiques—a copper kettle once used for making apple butter, an arborist's ladder, an Amish woodbin (now a coffee table)—evoke the rich history of the redesigned space.

Lighting Fixtures

In a home of period perfection, modern light fixtures can be jarring. Modern houses are often over-illuminated, especially by our ancestors' standards, and thereby lose a great deal of ambience. Try to save bright light for task areas, such as kitchen counters.

AVOID RECESSED DOWNLIGHTS

Keep lighting in the style of the house. Nothing announces a contemporary interior more than downlights set into the ceiling. While they are excellent for illuminating a room, they aren't as great at providing atmosphere. Instead, opt for wall sconces or graceful chandeliers. Experts recommend having five or so sources of light in a room, which will give it a natural feel and let you control the brightness. If you must use ceiling spots, choose halogen lights, which produce a warmer, more natural light than fluorescent or even tungsten fixtures do.

USE DIMMERS

You don't need maximum illumination at all times. Very often, a lower level of lighting is both practical and more attractive. In dining rooms, bedrooms, bathrooms, and even entrance halls, install dimmer switches. They allow you to adjust the light to suit the mood and the occasion.

HIDE WIRING

While a bulb can be made to resemble a candle flame, wires belie the facade. If possible, use sconces that have no electrical cords or run electrical cords along molding or trim where they blend into the woodwork. One devoted restorationist hid switchplates behind tiny doors in the woodwork and eliminated all table lamps.

MAKE YOUR OWN LAMPS

If you are lucky enough to find old glass lamps that once held kerosene or even whale oil, have them wired; they can go far in imparting a period mood (you can also find reproductions). Another option is to take old vases or other interesting containers (old crockery, for example) to a lighting store, which can convert them into distinctive lamps.

The Heritage
of a Home

For years, the Federal-style house was so dilapidated that it was known in its Westchester County, New York, neighborhood as the haunted house. It had been in the same family for generations; fortunately, none of them felt any inclination to alter it much. Floors, woodwork, and six fireplaces (several with marble mantels) were virtually as they had been in the mid-19th century. Fifteen years ago, a builder purchased the 1840 dwelling, restored it, and added a kitchen onto the back. The current owners

bought the home from him seven years ago and, benefiting from his efforts, made only a few cosmetic changes. These included lavishing the perfectly proportioned rooms with built-ins and shelves to hold their many books and collections, and painting the rooms in quietly elegant colors that highlight the home's intricate details.

The now gracious home (LEFT) features a circular driveway, generous porch, and four chimneys for its six fireplaces. In the entrance hall (OPPOSITE), glorious elements such as ten-foot ceilings, a stunning staircase, and original wide-plank floors are perfectly preserved. Although it did not come with the house, the bell-jar light is an antique. A coat closet was tucked into the space underneath the stairs.

Because the dining room faces east, the owners installed a mirror over the fireplace to bring even more light into the space (OPPOSITE). Almost every downstairs room has its own fireplace, enabling the homeowners to treat each one a little differently. Sometime in the past, several of the fireplaces were converted to gas heaters. Although the fireplaces are no longer functioning, the owners plan to convert them back to wood-burning ones in the near future. A beveled mirror made of old glass sits atop one of the marble mantels with an old photograph propped in front of it (ABOVE LEFT). "I am a connoisseur of jeweled fruit," says the husband referring to the more than 300 pineapples, oranges, bananas, pears, and peaches that sit in wire baskets on the new built-ins in his wife's home office (ABOVE RIGHT). The second-floor room was formerly a nursery.

The Kitchen

THERE IS A CERTAIN FREEDOM *inherent in remodeling the kitchen of an older*

home. No one expects a kitchen to be historically pure or for a homeowner to cook on

the hearth and carry water in from

the well. But as one homeowner put it,

there's no point in living in a period

home and having a kitchen that looks

like it was just built. Fortunately for

those people trying to blend modern

kitchen conveniences into a room rich

with the patina of age, the remodeling

71

industry has introduced countless products that are reproductions of— or inspired by—historical styles. Reproductions of vintage sinks, faucets, and pulls are readily available. Cabinetry now features many of the details and styles of older pieces—raised panels, beadboard, and decorative trim. Finishes can evoke the timeworn look of old paint. Take your cues from the architecture of the house: If you live in a barn with big oak beams, consider oak cabinets that are stained and weathered to echo the beams that inspired them. | Don't be afraid of texture. It adds interest and keeps a kitchen from looking too new. Slide-out baskets make wonderful storage bins,

unpainted brick hearkens back to earlier times, and

a smattering of hand-painted tiles lends the touch of

an artisan. In fact, anything handcrafted will help

create a warm, old-fashioned mood. │ Details are

key. While you may not wish to hide every outlet

(although you can—behind false drawer fronts

that tilt open), modern necessities can be dis-

guised. To minimize their presence, panel appli-

ance fronts to match the cabinetry, and organize

smaller appliances behind roll-up doors.

An Homage to the Past

All the must-haves of a contemporary kitchen can be found in this brand-new room that was produced for a designer show-house—an efficient floor plan, easy-to-clean surfaces, plentiful storage, room to dine, and abundant light. But much of it would not appear out of place in an 18th- or 19th-century home, for it borrows the best qualities from the past and merely improves upon them.

The soft, pale colors are certainly modern. Yet many of the elements hearken back to yesteryear, beginning with the sweeping arches that define the space. One arch envelops the range and evokes an old cooking hearth; another defines the eating area and recalls the flying buttresses of ancient cathedrals. The classic recessed-panel cabinetry is crafted in a light wood with reproduction Victorian pulls and traditional beadboard insets. Instead of floor-to-ceiling banks of cabinetry, there are plenty of open shelves that run from the windows to the cooking alcove. Supported by decorative brackets (similar to those on the exterior of Victorian houses), the shelves provide an opportunity for displaying a collection of vintage kitchenware, and also hide the small lights that illuminate the countertops.

A new home doesn't have to feel too new. Beadboard plays its part in bringing character to this new kitchen in the recessed panels of the cabinetry and on the backsplash. Texture comes from slate on the stove-flanking countertops; the remainder of the counters are the same pale wood as the cupboards. The architect installed an inexpensive rod across the top of the range to serve as a convenient pot rack, where pots and pans hanging from metal hooks stay within easy reach of the cook. A palette of soothing, cool colors unifies the room.

Architectural and decorative elements separate dining and cooking areas without cutting them off or blocking views. The removal of a load-bearing wall was turned into an architectural asset—buttresses and a support beam join to form one arch. A matching arch defines the cooking area. Different flooring materials—hardwood and stone-like tile—reinforce the distinction between the spaces.

Natural materials always evoke the past. A large apron sink (ABOVE LEFT), made from rough-hewn Vermont soapstone, complements the adjacent slate countertops. The island's countertop (ABOVE RIGHT) is crafted of pale butcher-block in the same hue as the cabinets. A second sink in the island augments the work triangle and lets two cooks work simultaneously. White appliances such as the two curved-glass wall ovens, and a refrigerator with a panel that matches the cupboards, blend into the rest of the room. Though built in, the lighted storage cabinet (OPPOSITE) was designed to resemble an old kitchen hutch.

Living History

J ust like a great view or a stunning piece of architecture, a house with a past has an irresistible appeal. A three-story structure in New York, occupied by British forces during the American Revolution, had been in the same family since it was built in 1757. When the present homeowners bought it, they inherited a pedigree, but one that came with a cramped 1960s kitchen. As part of a total restoration of the house and grounds, the family added on this roomy new kitchen in what had been a roofed overhang. To ease the transition between the addition and the rest of the house, they used some salvaged pieces (the oak island was once a counter in a hardware store), some recycled (they kept the original five-foot-wide farm-house sink), and rich woods that could have been a part of the house's earlier life.

To match the adjoining room's original flooring, the owners milled down 100-year-old fir boards from an old factory. Cherry-stained beadboard sheathes the ceiling (LEFT). The island's drawers (RIGHT) were fashioned from old barn wood.

False drawer fronts disguise a pair of side-by-side dishwashers so they blend visually with neighboring functional drawers (LEFT). The refrigerator (OPPOSITE) sports a historical facade as well: Its panels recall a vintage compartmentalized icebox. It's not a coincidence: Hinges and latches salvaged from a genuine icebox discovered on the property were added to the new panels. There's a lesson to be learned here: Even though a piece may appear damaged beyond repair, rescued wood and hardware can easily enhance new furnishings and appliances. Vintage details also help create an authentic ambience—an old scale and vintage storage tins stand out against the beadboard backsplash.

Adding Storage

You can never have too much storage in the kitchen—the one part of the house where form and function must complement each other. Well-thought-out storage space can mean the difference between a frustrating and a pleasurable cooking experience.

ASSESS YOUR NEEDS

One trick is to take out everything that is stored in your present kitchen and put it in piles on the floor. This way you'll know exactly what you need space for, and if you need specialized space such as room for tall cereal boxes or cookie sheets. Think hard about how you live—whether you shop daily or once a week, for example. Your habits will dictate your storage needs.

PUT IT WHERE YOU NEED IT

Plan to store items as close as possible to the counter or the appliance where you use them.

■ Place dish storage near the dishwasher and close to the table.

■ Hang spice racks close to the range.

■ Put specialized storage—such as appliance garages or cookbook shelves—at a convenient height (you don't want to bend down to get a blender, for example).

■ Place seldom-used objects, such as the turkey platter for Thanksgiving dinner, up high.

MAKE EVERY SQUARE INCH WORK

Claim every bit of unused space. Corners can house lazy Susans, a slim shelf along the backsplash can hold spices, shelves a mere 8 inches deep can house cookbooks at the end of an island. Shallow shelves—no more than one jam-jar in depth—can also be slipped into many places. To claim even more space, get rid of soffits that rarely serve any purpose, and put in cupboards that stretch to the ceiling for less frequently used items.

MIX IT UP

Break up a monotonous wall of cabinetry with a mix of glass-fronted cupboards, open shelves, and other elements such as plate and wine racks. More than just places to stash things, these areas let you brighten and personalize your kitchen by displaying favorite pottery or other collectibles.

Rags
To Riches

The old maxim "one man's trash is another man's treasure," is one this homeowner lives by. Virtually everything in his 1912 farmhouse in upstate New York is a cast-off. His philosophy enabled him to update the kitchen—which was dark and gloomy and had last been touched in the 1970s—relatively inexpensively. The owner painted the cupboards white, changed the handles, added a secondhand plate rack, and sanded and refinished the original knotty-pine floor. To reverse an earlier, poorly done insulating job that had left numerous patches on the walls, the owner added thin sheets of drywall. Because everything looked too new afterwards, he decided not to paint the doors, which looked ravaged after the 1970s paneling was ripped off. He felt they gave the finished kitchen a much-needed timeworn touch.

In the pantry (LEFT), a circa-1880 buffet provides storage. The shapely 1920s Magic Chef stove (RIGHT) was found discarded at a mansion in Long Island. The island came from a long-shuttered restaurant, as did the Pammer House sign.

This homeowner knows well the power of white paint. He has used it liberally throughout to unify his disparate furnishings. The breakfast nook's table and bench (OPPOSITE) came from a junk shop and probably were a part of a summer cottage's kitchenette. The owner simply painted them white. The salvaged office chair was slip-covered white to match. In the dining room (RIGHT), a grouping of enamelware sits atop a buffet found at another junk shop. White paint revitalized it, along with the lyre-backed dining chairs and table, which were free cast-offs.

A Pedigree
of Its Own

A passion for cooking and entertaining inspired the homeowners of an elegant Federal-style home in Long Island, New York, to transform several tiny rooms (including an upstairs loft and bathroom) into this light-filled kitchen. Their challenge was to make the kitchen reflect the quiet elegance of the rest of the house and not reveal its lack of pedigree.

Their solution: materials that either have a past or hint at one. Rich cherry cabinetry with simple round knobs echoes cherry antiques in nearby rooms. Whenever possible, the owners selected salvaged materials to bring a sense of age to the new room. A "witch's elbow" fireplace was crafted from antique bricks and has a bluestone hearth, while the floors were made from old yellow-pine planks. Even the French doors are recycled. They date to 1850 and were salvaged from a house in Staten Island, New York.

Gracious but unassuming, the 1832 sea captain's house (LEFT) had remained in the same family for more than 150 years. Removing two upstairs rooms enabled the owners to raise the kitchen ceiling high, resulting in an airy and inviting space (OPPOSITE) that has become the heart of the home.

Old Wood Floors

Imagine a new floor with the patina and character of antique wood. You can have it, by using old, salvaged timber. Such reclaimed wood is the ultimate in recycling; no trees are cut down and wood that at one time would have been left to rot is put to good use.

Salvaged timber generally comes from old barns, mills, or warehouses. This wood is usually heart pine or, more rarely, chestnut, or red or white oak. It features beautiful grain, and worm or nail holes. And it comes in hues not found in new timber. A smaller amount of reclaimed wood is actually recovered from ponds, rivers, and lakes—wood that was logged many years ago but never made it to the mill.

Some paint techniques books give formulas for "aging" new or freshly sanded floors. Achieving an even and convincing effect requires some skill and involves trial and error, so experiment on scrap wood before you embark on an entire room.

CONSIDER COST

The one downside to reclaimed wood is its price—it can cost several times as much as new wood floors and, since it often comes in irregular widths and thicknesses, it can be much more expensive to install.

ASK FOR A HISTORY

Many dealers in old timber provide information on where the wood came from and how old it is. If you love the look of lots of different boards and can't decide, make your choice based on the story behind them.

CHOOSE OLD WOOD

No matter how much you pay for modern wood floors, old floors will be stronger. This is because the trees in America's virgin forests were much larger than those logged today, so they produced wider planks. Furthermore, the crowded growing conditions in those forests caused the wood to grow slowly and produce a very dense heartwood (up to 30 growth rings per square inch as opposed to four to seven in present-day trees). That means floors that can handle water, insects, and foot traffic far better than contemporary wood floors.

The Warmth
of White

A homely 1960s kitchen was the only unlovely aspect of the gorgeous red-brick 1871 Italianate dwelling in Ohio. For the husband and wife who bought it, updating the kitchen was their first priority. They were able to leave the walls and long windows in their original positions, but had to remove two false ceilings that had been put in by previous owners in order to regain the original, lofty 11-foot ceiling. Then they commissioned a local cabinetmaker to create an entire wall of cabinetry using multipaned doors that the couple unearthed at a salvage yard. Incorporated into the cabinetry was an old humidor that once displayed tobacco products in a general store. To engender an ethereal, airy feeling and to unify the old and new cabinets and the entire space, the couple painted everything a rich, creamy white. Rather than disguise the modern appliances, they chose to use their stainless exteriors as an accent to the white.

Vintage wrought-iron fencing frames the elegant home's tiny lot (LEFT). The broad columned porch— which needed only minor repairs and repainting— provides the perfect spot for watching the small town's Fourth of July parade. In the kitchen (OPPOSITE), the couple preserved the hefty original window molding when they gutted the room. Because the kitchen looks out over the garden, they chose double-hung windows without mullions so they have a clear view of the backyard. Creamy walls and cabinets, and stainless accents, keep the space looking warm but also sleek and professional.

The duo kept costs
down by opting for a
stainless-steel cart in lieu of
an expensive custom-built
island. They simply wheel it
where needed. Several pieces
of Victorian ironstone sit
above the state-of-the-art
stainless steel range. To make
the cabinetry appear unfitted,
the owners did not take it all
the way up to the ceiling. The
cupboards end a few inches
below it. The tiny cubbies
with exposed dovetail joints
were custom made. While
the pendant lights are new,
the center light was taken
from an old schoolhouse.
Ironstone eggcups do double
duty as vases for roses.

Sweet Homecoming

Dorothy, of *The Wizard of Oz* fame, would have felt right at home in this farmhouse. Located just outside of Omaha, the turn-of-the-20th-century house is surrounded by towering shade trees and a perennial garden of hollyhocks, lilacs, and peonies. The daughter who inherited it completed its most recent restoration. She remembers well her parents making the building livable back in the 1950s. "I can still picture my mother, in rolled-up jeans and a red bandana in her hair, pushing wheelbarrow after wheelbarrow full of old bricks up the hill," she recalls. After her parents passed away, the daughter decided to bring the home back to life.

The kitchen needed close attention: It was a cramped space with little natural light. "There was light coming in," she says. "But 1950s light, not modern light." To remedy the space problem, the remodeling crew tore out an island and took over an adjacent mudroom to form a large open work space. To brighten things up, they added a bank of windows over the new sink. Fancy cabinets crafted from costly woods would have looked out of place in the down-to-earth farmhouse. Instead, the owner chose beadboard cupboards painted white, with old-fashioned nickel pulls.

The kitchen captures the informal spirit of the Nebraska farmhouse. To update it, the owner picked thoroughly modern colors—celery, French blue, and mustard brown. Cabinets with glass fronts and sides show off a grouping of colorful enamelware, which the homeowner gathered from antiquing forays around the country. To add more open display space, the cupboards stop a good six inches below the ceiling. A small lip on the back of the countertop provides the perfect space for displaying prints or photographs.

The owner's favorite aspect of the house is the comforting view of the barns from the long bank of windows installed over the sink. Claiming center stage is a dramatic and eye-catching 1860s Dutch table that serves as an island. A vintage farrier's toolbox is tucked beneath it. New beadboard on the ceiling complements the beadboard cabinets.

Countertops
and Islands

Beyond the traditional tile, granite, butcher
block, and solid surfacing, countertop choices
now include concrete, slate, limestone, and
unexpected woods such as mahogany. Select
materials that are appropriate for your house.
For instance, for a kitchen in an 1890 Queen
Anne—style house, glossy black granite may
be in order, while green tile may be more
fitting for an Arts-and-Crafts bungalow.
Always check the cost of installation before
selecting a countertop, and think about
issues such as durability and maintenance.

The indispensable island provides
storage, counter space, and an eating place.
It also offers an area where non-cooks can
linger without getting in the way of the
chef, who will most likely be within the work
triangle—the area defined by the sink, stove,
and refrigerator.

ASK ABOUT UPKEEP

Some countertop materials require
more care than others. Certain woods
(such as mahogany) need regular paste
waxing; concrete should be treated
with a sealant every six months;
limestone will stain, particularly if
liquids such as lemon juice or wine
are not wiped up right away.

CONSIDER CONCRETE

Concrete has come off the sidewalk
and into the kitchen. Incredibly sturdy
and versatile, it can be poured and
dyed to resemble virtually any stone
(and is cheaper to install than granite
or marble), and of course it can be
built to suit almost any space or
shape. Because it comes in liquid form,
interesting objects or patterns can be
put into it. Some homeowners
decorate theirs with seashells, while
others opt to put their kids' handprints
in their countertops.

AN ISLAND APART

The island can dictate the look of the kitchen. For a real farmhouse air, or if you are using the island in an old house as a bridge between a new kitchen and other rooms, transform a vintage table or a large piece of old wood or butcher block into an island. For a more modern style, or if your kitchen is cramped, you may want to opt for an inexpensive two-tier wheeled butcher-block or stainless-steel cart that can be moved.

Make the island distinctive by painting or staining it a different color than the rest of the cabinetry, or by using another countertop material.

MULTIPLE WORK STATIONS

If you have the room and anticipate several cooks working at once, create two or even three work triangles. Add a small prep sink to an island, install a refrigerator drawer for vegetables beside it, or, if there is a baker in the house, put in a section of marble for rolling and handling dough.

A Getaway for a Gourmet

As co-founder of New York City's gourmet food emporium Dean & DeLuca, this homeowner craved a weekend cottage that was truly an escape from the hustle and bustle of the big city. Not surprisingly, the design of the kitchen was of utmost importance. "I wanted a soothing, easy-care environment with a few fun touches," he explains.

The home he found, a charming 1929 bungalow in East Hampton, New York, suited his purposes exactly. Fortunately, the kitchen needed only to be updated. First, he covered the walls with smooth and shiny subway tiles, which eliminated the need for backsplashes. To the upper cabinets of frosted glass and wood trim, he added stainless-steel bottom cabinets and a combination of butcher block and granite countertops. Color and pattern are kept to the bare minimum, no blinds cover the window (privacy was not an issue), and no decorative tiles interrupt the expanse of white tiled walls. Maintenance is kept to a minimum: Every surface—including the walls—can be wiped down and cleaned in a flash, which is just what he wanted. Since he often entertains informally here, he made it a goal to create a "serviceable—not fashionable and impractical—kitchen: One that works for me."

The owner's changes in the kitchen were mostly cosmetic. Subway tile replaced outdated wallpaper; the existing window, which overlooks the garden, was left curtainless. To link the hanging cupboards with a Stickley bookcase in the dining room, the owner had them crafted in that style. He then added frosted glass panes. A rolling metal cart, topped with wood, functions as an island on wheels. Food is the star of this kitchen; the architecture is merely background. Even the stainless-steel cabinets have unassuming metal pulls.

Inspiration for the space came from no-nonsense restaurant kitchens. There is nothing fussy or extra here. Stainless-steel countertops flank the professional-quality range and simplify cooking and cleanup. An eclectic mix of French and American ceramicware is kept on hand in recessed shelving.

Painting Floors

*In Colonial America, rugs—like wallpaper—
were costly and out of reach for most people.
Hence the painted floor. It injected color
and pattern into a room and had the added
benefit of hiding dirt. Floors were either
stenciled or painted freehand in motifs
ranging from checkerboard to graining to
marbleizing. Today, a painted floor can
be an intriguing touch that has the added
benefit of being easy—and inexpensive—
to change. If you get tired of it, you simply
paint over it. As for care, painted floors need
only sweeping and the occasional damp
mop. They are particularly great for the
kitchen or dining room where rugs often get
stained from spilled food or liquids.*

PAINT YOUR OWN DIAMOND-PATTERNED FLOOR:

1. Measure the entire floor. Map out the complete pattern on a piece of grid paper at a scale of one inch equals one foot. Diamonds measuring 8 to 12 inches square will resemble marble tile most closely, but any size will do.

2. Transfer a diamond, drawn to scale, onto a template of thick cardboard.

3. Sand and clean the floor.

4. Choose two colors of paint. To mimic traditional marble tile floors, use black and white. Otherwise, if you want the floor to claim center stage, paint it in starkly contrasting colors. For a more subtle appearance, choose colors that are more closely related, such as gray and cream. Both oil and latex paint will work; remember that oil dries more slowly but is much more durable and better-looking. Paint the entire floor with the base-coat color (it should be the lightest hue). Let it dry for at least 24 hours.

5. Using a pencil and hard-edged rule, mark out the pattern. Start at the middle of the room, centering the most prominent sequence of diamonds, then work out toward the edges.

6. With painter's tape, mark off the interior edges of alternating diamonds, making sure that the tape aligns with the pencil line. Press the tape down firmly so that no paint seeps under it.

7. Using a brush or a small roller, paint every other diamond in a hue that contrasts with the base color. Let the floor dry.

8. Apply three coats of polyurethane for protection, sanding between coats. If you want the floor to weather fast, don't put polyurethane on it at all. Just apply a coat of paste wax.

The Bathroom

IT HAS NEVER BEEN EASIER *to imbue bathrooms with personal style. A wide*

variety of sinks, tubs, tiles, and hardware gives homeowners choices they've never had

before. Whether the room you are tackling is a tiny powder room or a master bath,

the cardinal rule remains the same: Keep the

space appropriate for the house. | *In an old or*

old-style house, this means giving the room

vintage distinction while keeping it highly

functional and, equally important, preserving

a comfortable environment. Anything that

adds some character is a plus—a flea market

sideboard (nothing too valuable) turned into a vanity with a sink put into it, antique accessories like a silver baby cup to hold toothbrushes. Hang mirrors judiciously; they can expand a room visually and make it sparkle. Recess as many storage

spaces as possible, including hampers, but add one freestanding piece, whether it be an old painted chair or a slim storage cupboard to store towels and soaps. Consider wood floors, which, while not as versatile as tile, lend enormous character. If sealed or painted properly, a wood

floor should be as durable

as tile. Use floor mats

around the tub or shower

and clean up standing water immediately. | Illumination is very important in a

bathroom, so try to have several lighting sources. Augment the overall lighting with task

lighting for specific areas. Dimmers are an easy but important add-on as well. They

can be adjusted to create a relaxing mood, or to accommodate reading in the tub. | In

a small bath you should aim to keep the palette simple. Follow the advice of experts

and stick with white or cream fixtures. Nothing dates a room as quickly as colored

fixtures. Instead rely on paint, paper, fabric, and accessories to set the style of your bath.

Humble Origins, Grand Results

Although every square inch of a rambling home on eastern Long Island, New York, is new, it has the spirit of a farmhouse that has been lived in for generations. The sense of antiquity carries through to the master bathroom via traditional—and modest—materials. But while the materials may call to mind the past, the way they have been used is utterly modern. Taking her cue from old work tables, the homeowner had a furniture maker craft the double-bowl vanity from recycled wood, adding a galvanized

steel top—an unexpected touch. Distressed paint disguises the medicine cabinets as well-worn mirrors and evokes the painted folk furnishings that decorate the rest of the house. Nothing is too fancy; every fixture and surface is streamlined. Colors are neutral and white predominates. "I wanted a look that was spare but not austere," says the homeowner.

Personality abounds in this bathroom thanks to the homeowner's innovative use of humble classic materials. Above an antique iron tub and around the perimeter of the room (LEFT), smooth stones gathered from walks along the beach line the ledge of the white beadboard. Even though she knew it would require upkeep, the owner put a galvanized steel top on the custom vanity (RIGHT). Because it stains easily, she wipes it down after each use. Below, square wicker baskets hold various bathroom supplies. In addition to the two uplight sconces, there is a ceiling light for overall illumination.

Bathroom Planning

*Before you undertake a redo of your
bathroom, consider all the little frustrations
that test your patience in your current space.
Is the towel always just out of reach when
you step out of the shower? Are you applying
makeup or shaving in shadow? Is a fresh box
of tissues in the closet down the hall? Does
the entire space steam up with every shower?
Making out a list of problems as well as a
wish list will help your architect or designer
pinpoint major flaws, as well as help you
determine where to put your money. If you
want to use period fixtures, select them
before deciding on the layout of the room,
as they do not always conform to standard
measurements.While you may spend less
time in the bathroom, planning it is just as
important as planning your kitchen.*

MAKE SOME SPACE

In most bathrooms you need to grab
storage where you can. As with the
kitchen, think of all you really want to
keep at hand. Build in a tall cabinet for
towel storage or, if you have room,
put in a freestanding piece of furniture
like an armoire. Don't forget the wall
above the toilet. Open shelves, or—if
planned ahead—a recessed cabinet
often fit perfectly there. Baskets made
of rattan, wicker, or wire can hold
books, bath products, cleaning
supplies, or washcloths. Furthermore, a
mix of materials lends charm to a room
known for its hard surfaces. Don't
forget hooks—especially for kids'
baths—they take up little space and
make hanging wet towels a snap.

PUT FUNCTION FIRST

Reflect on how the bathroom will be
used before you consider style. If two
people get ready for work or school
at once, put in two sinks and tuck
the toilet in an alcove for privacy. If
someone needs to sit down and apply
makeup, install a low vanity with a
stool. If you and your partner are tall,
opt for a vanity instead of a freestanding sink: It's easy to build the
cabinet to the height you need. Or, if
you are working on a kids' bathroom,
consider dark or gray grout for tiles—
dirt won't show as readily.

A Boatbuilder's Beauty

This master bathroom
(OPPOSITE) may be brand new,
but its components lend it a
timeless air. The fine detailing
on the linen closet, the window
surround, and the curved
ceiling recall the workmanship
of an earlier era. Both the
sink and the faucet are stylish
reproductions that look
the part. Rather than inject
permanent color in the
soothing all-white setting, the
owner brings it in with
old-fashioned sky-blue seltzer
bottles that catch the light
from the window. A porcelain-
lined soap holder (RIGHT) rests
on the edge of the sink.

The bathroom in a rather grand Italianate home in Ohio left much to be desired. It was small and dated, so the owner claimed it and an adjoining closet to form a new master bathroom. His design goal: to have a bathroom that would keep its newness under wraps and meld seamlessly with the rest of the home. For help, he tapped an Ohio cabinetmaker who is also a boatbuilder. The carpenter introduced some nautical touches, including a vaulted ceiling that resembles an inverted ship's hull (the attic lies above) and the cabinetry's flush-mounted ring pulls. Other boat-inspired elements: the oversized towel hook, the lamp over the mirror, and the ceiling light. To

complete the deception of age, the owner laid hexagonal tiles on the floor and used traditional subway tile on the walls and tub surround. As decorative touches, the owner, who collects architectural salvage, put a pair of diminutive antique columns in the window as well as a period corbel to support his stereo speaker.

Every renovation involves trade-offs, and this one was no exception. Because the linen closet was incorporated into the new space, storage space had to be created elsewhere. The owner gave up a freestanding shower (settling instead for a shower/tub combination) in order to get sizable cabinets (LEFT) within the bathroom. The flush-mounted ring pulls give the cabinets a particularly streamlined appearance.

The sink top (OPPOSITE) stays clutter-free, thanks to an ingenious tree that has bars for washcloths and twistable trays (which double as mirrors) for holding necessities. Running vertically, the tree takes up very little space.

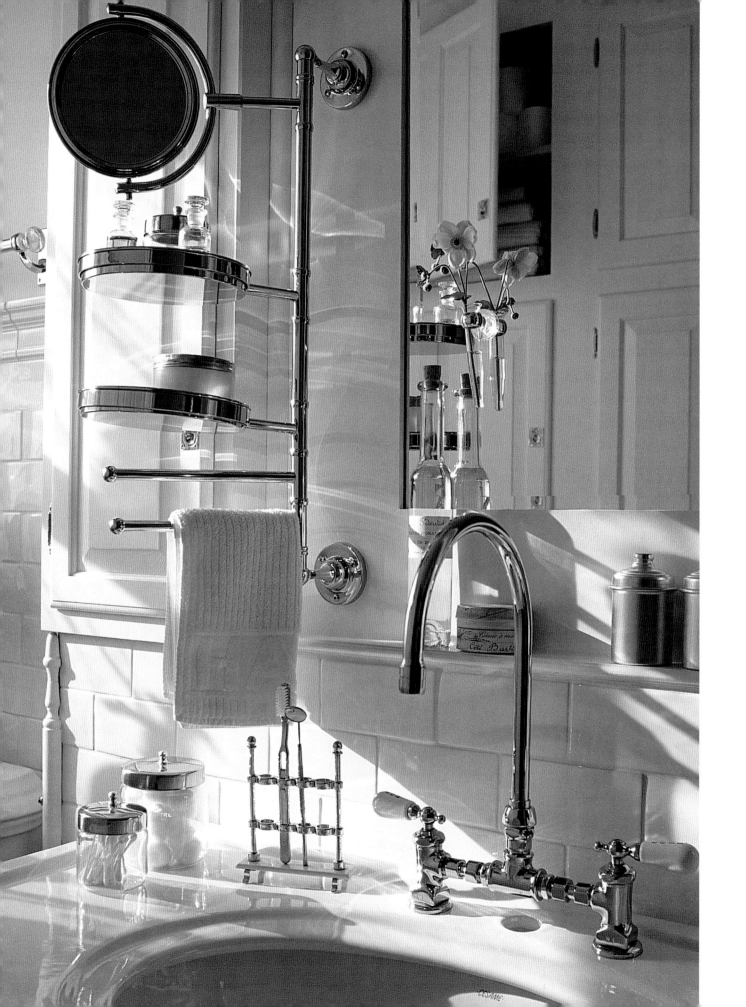

From Salvage to Stardom

Although the farmhouse was built in 1977, it appeared so genuinely 19th-century that not even the real estate agent showing it to the two prospective buyers knew its true provenance. "Until we looked at the basement beams we never realized that it was a modern house," says one of the buyers. "It was done very convincingly." Sadly, the man who built the house never quite completed it; from the appearance of the bathroom it seemed as if he had literally run out of money in the middle of construction. A pink plastic Roman tub sat in the center of the room, but there was no toilet, no sink, no woodwork. The wallpaper reached only halfway up the walls.

The two new owners, who bought the house at a foreclosure sale, are antiques dealers with a love of salvage materials. They put in a reproduction tub, which they tucked behind three old doors fashioned into a screen. They hung a cast-iron mirror—salvaged from a bank and with its original beveled glass—above the sink. To create the sink, they cut a Victorian drainpipe in two for legs and topped them with an 80-year-old marble basin that they had had reglazed. They measured the openings carefully and then chose reproduction fixtures from a catalog that specializes in old-fashioned faucets.

Beadboard carried halfway up the wall conveys a sense of age in this master bathroom. The owners chose the wallpaper for its resemblance to hand-painted stripes. To hang the 150-pound mirror, they had to secure two mollies into the wall. Because the mirror takes the place of a medicine cabinet, bathroom necessities are stored in a Victorian trunk stowed underneath the sink.

Rather than partitioning the bathroom, the owners sheltered the free-standing tub with a screen constructed from old French doors that they bought at auction. They scraped the dirt off the panels but chose not to replace the missing glass lozenges. In lieu of refinishing the pine floors, they opted to cover them in four coats of water-proof marine deck paint. With a linen closet down the hall, they saw no need for one in the bathroom. An antique wrought-iron garden chair does the duty, holding a stack of folded towels.

Reglazing and Using Old Fixtures

Because reproduction fixtures now are so well made and attractive, and because technology has improved many fixtures, it usually makes sense to spend the money for new ones if you are doing a major bathroom overhaul. However, if you are simply updating your bathroom cosmetically, refinishing your existing sink or bathtub can be a good way to save money. It will give you the chance to change that avocado green sink to a fresh, clean white; if you prefer, you can have the refinisher custom-match the color to a curtain fabric or other fixture, too.

REGLAZE THE ORIGINAL

If you are investing in a new bathroom, you should really love an item before you spend money to refinish it, especially if it is deeply pitted (pits are difficult to remove). Otherwise, view this as an opportunity to get a larger or more luxurious version. Restoring the enamel on a tub or sink is a good option if you have a great-looking vintage model, or if you just want to make the existing bathtub or sink look more presentable by smoothing over a rough surface or eliminating rust stains. For the average job, reglazing is not expensive, it takes about a day, and is done on the premises. The typical reglazing will last about five to ten years.

OPT FOR NEW FAUCETS

As tempting as that cheap faucet is at the tag sale or salvage yard, you are probably better off buying a new one. Chances are, you won't have all the parts and won't know it until the plumber is at your house trying in vain to install the faucet. In addition, faucet technology has improved immeasurably. Gone are the rubber washers that needed to be replaced so often; today's faucets have ceramic cartridges, which require almost no maintenance and last almost forever.

Bed and Bath

Become One

Often in the Victorian era an extended family lived under one roof, which explains why houses from that time have so many little rooms—builders were trying to give each person a bedroom, no matter how tiny. Although this Ohio house dates to 1915, its interior was decidedly Victorian (technically, the Victorian era ended in 1901). "There was quite a bit of space, but it was broken up in weird ways," says one of the homeowners. To create a sense of spaciousness in the master bedroom, the couple removed a dividing wall between two small bedrooms to form an open bedroom/bathroom. A small dressing area is stepped up behind the sleeping space and is separated from it by a partial wall. The dressing area leads to the bathroom proper, where the toilet is tucked into its own space behind a door. Together with the owners' intriguing collection of salvaged pieces, the result is an informal yet distinctive space.

The couple's contractor rescued a classic 1910 sink (OPPOSITE) from another job and custom-built the cabinet around it. Because both the husband and wife are tall, he made it four feet high so they wouldn't have to bend down. Beadboard, a reproduction faucet, and old glass knobs make the new piece appear vintage. A mirror from a defunct barber shop fits above the sink perfectly. The primitive twig table beside it still has its original paint. Straw hats hang on antique hooks on a piece of old decorative molding reborn as an attractive curio shelf (LEFT).

By opening the bedroom and bath to one another (ABOVE), the owners made the entire area feel more roomy and gracious. Because the wall removed was load-bearing, the contractor added a steel-beam ceiling and left a partial wall. The owners believe strongly in the power of white paint. They "aged" the new bed by painting it white and then distressing it. A similar technique improved a bedside table found at an antiques shop. A trio of rescued brackets look almost sculptural on the wall, as does an ornate corbel unearthed in a salvage yard. In the bathroom (OPPOSITE), wire locker baskets from a gym hold towels and support a houseplant. The owners found the cupboards in the garage and had their contractor rebuild them; they were likely part of the original kitchen. A section of lattice serves as a towel holder and forms a quiet design in the almost pattern-free room.

Choosing Tile

There's a reason tile has remained popular since the time of the Roman Empire. It's versatile, durable, beautiful, water resistant, relatively inexpensive, and easy to clean. All of which makes it the perfect choice for bathroom walls, floors, and countertops. If your house has its original tile, be sure to clean it first before you decide to pull it up. You may change your mind after you've scrubbed it with a mild abrasive cleanser and warm water. Even if you dislike the tile color but it is in good shape, you can still repaint it using a special epoxy paint.

The most common size of tile is four-by-four inches. But larger sizes—such as eight-by-eight, ten-by-ten, and twelve-by-twelve—are becoming more popular. Never out of favor are clean-lined subway tiles—rectangular glossy tiles laid like bricks—that look appropriate in any period house.

CHECK OUT OFF-THE-RACK FIRST

Don't immediately head for the custom tile section. You can save money and get a truly individual look by using standard tile. Many tile patterns come in sets that include trim tiles. Use these given combinations, or mix and match your own. Use different colors to make a pattern, or employ standard tiles as a backdrop for a smattering of custom-made art tiles. One simple but effective strategy is to create a giant diamond of tiles within a tile floor. Yet another is to use grout in a contrasting color (dark grout has the added advantage of hiding dirt).

AVOID TRENDS

At one time, harvest gold and avocado green bathrooms were the height of fashion; now they just look dated. Remember that when you pick out a trendy pattern or color. Tile is difficult and costly to remove, so stick to patterns and colors that you believe will stand the test of time.

TRICK THE EYE

Use tile to alter the perception of space in your bathroom.

■ Place tiles on the diagonal to make a small room appear more spacious, or use oversized tiles in a mid-sized bathroom for a similar effect.

■ To create the illusion of width, add a horizontal band of contrasting tile around the walls.

■ To visually add height, try a vertical band in a contrasting color.

■ To bring elegance to an enclosed shower, install eye-catching trim around the outside frame of the door.

■ Give your bath an old-world aura by laying mosaic tiles underfoot. Because they are so small and have many grout lines, they are skid-resistant and therefore a good choice for the floor of the entire room or just the shower. Keep glossy tiles off the floor, however. Unglazed or low-glaze tiles will make the surface less slippery.

Old-World Grace, New-World Fit

The homeowners know the history of their Bedford, New York, home well. It was built in 1757 as a country home for a wealthy New York banker, and was then completely remodeled in 1880. When the couple renovated the master bathroom, they successfully created a Victorian-style bath that did not lack any modern conveniences. They matched white-glazed rectangular tiles on the wall and matte-finish hexagonal shower-floor tiles to examples from the Victorian era. Via the Internet, they found a company in Carrara, Italy, that crafted the not-standard one-by-two-foot marble floor tiles for a fraction of what they would have cost had they been cut in the United States. The same Italian company produced the double sink to the specifications of the owners, who took their inspiration from the single marble sinks found in other bathrooms in the house. The sink legs were crafted by a company that specializes in producing brass rails for bars. To add a touch of luxury, the couple opted for a towel warmer as well as radiant heat on the floors beneath the marble. For practical purposes they chose the electrical rather than the hot-water form of radiant heat; a leak in the hot-water version could be difficult to locate and would probably require tearing up the entire floor to fix.

Classical elements such as the column details and the arch above the recessed shelves lend old-fashioned grace to the new bathroom. Interestingly, the house had the first interior bathroom with running water in town. It was installed in 1920. The other bathrooms in the house date to the 1940s. During the renovation, the homeowners saved and reused all the original sinks.

A search for a double marble sink proved fruitless, so the owners had one made in Carrara, Italy (OPPOSITE). The legs are made of nickel-plated brass to the owners' specifications. Built-in medicine cabinets were designed and crafted by their carpenter to resemble old pieces. The shower unit was found at a salvage store. It was so cheap that the home-owners wouldn't have lost much if their plumber failed to fit it in. The towel warmer (RIGHT) is the one distinctly modern touch in the room; on the scale of indulgences, the homeowners say they actually enjoy the heated floor more. An antique rocking chair brings character and contrast to the all-white setting.

Decorating
the Bathroom

Bathrooms, often neglected and hard-edged spaces, benefit most from personal touches. Remember that this room can often be the perfect location to display some quirky flea market treasure or collection.

ADD COLLECTIBLES AND ART

Nothing personalizes a room like a grouping of treasures.

■ Display a collection of perfume bottles on a lighted shelf.

■ Use photographs or a painting to lend beauty to the bath. For impact in a small bath, line one wall, ceiling to floor, with photographs or prints all framed identically.

■ Clusters of mirrors, even new inexpensive mirrors, can make an impact. They augment the light in a room and create the illusion of space.

■ Rough-hewn pottery in earth tones brings warmth to a bathroom.

■ Remember, old collections, mirrors, or artwork don't need to be valuable to be eye-catching; in fact, it is best if they aren't valuable since they will be exposed to the moisture of a bathroom. Scour flea markets or tag sales for old photos and vintage frames.

INSTALL ARCHITECTURE

A wall of beadboard, a thick line of crown molding along the ceiling, a slim shelf, or simply a picture rail helps to make a bathroom feel more inviting and look less like a laboratory.

DON'T FORGET FURNITURE

Against the sleek surfaces of a bath-room, a venerable piece injects a punch of contrast. Just one is all it takes: A crusty painted mirror, a quirky bookshelf, or a vintage wrought-iron chair will each lend character. If you have the room, add more. Forego the medicine cabinet and hang a mirror instead. If possible, cabinetry should resemble furniture as well. Choose a vanity with the attributes of a fine dressing table and dress it up further with unusual knobs.

BRIGHTEN WITH COLOR

As soothing as all-white is, colorful walls can add warmth to a large bathroom. And in a small one, color can jazz up the look. Despite the old adage that diminutive spaces require light walls, a rich deep hue on the walls will actually make a bathroom feel more intimate and cozy. And, by painting ceiling and walls the same shade, awkward angles—so common in many upstairs baths—will be diminished.

Bold shots of colors are another trick. Enliven all-white surroundings with stacks of solid-color towels. Even vases filled with fresh flowers will assume additional impact when set in a pristine white bath.

SOFTEN THE FLOOR

A colorful rag rug, or better yet a small Oriental carpet, will do wonders for the appearance of a bathroom; and they have the added benefit of making the floor warmer underfoot. Just be sure to place a no-skid pad underneath.

House **Exteriors**

CURB APPEAL: IT IS THE SIREN SONG *of old houses that first*

lures us in and captivates us. Whether it is the pleasing proportions of a Georgian-style

house or the rustic simplicity of a log cabin, there is something about a venerable dwelling

that draws the eye. | *Sadly for many houses,*

the exteriors have been altered either through

neglect or by a misguided desire to make them

look like something other than what they are.

For instance, porches often rotted off houses or

were removed in the mid-20th century to give

a house a more "modern" appearance. By the

same token, plain-lined Colonial homes were frequently

tarted up with details such as gables and Victorian ginger-

bread. You may like some of the past changes, or may be unable to undo them, but you

need to understand them. The first step in

returning an exterior to the height of its beau-

ty is detective work. | Unless your home is the

only surviving example from a specific period,

there are probably others like it nearby. Look

around for similar structures, get books on

architectural periods, or see if the local histor-

ical society has old photographs of your house. One homeowner never understood why his four chimneys were so tall—until he saw a picture of his house that showed a third story. So, look for aspects of your house that seem "off." Chances are they are a later change, or an alteration by default. | Follow general restoration guidelines: Make changes after you've done your research and had the house inspected by an expert. Go slowly. Sometimes things are revealed over time. And try to put additions on the back, so the front of the house will remain unchanged for future generations.

Exterior Colors

Few home decisions are as nerve-wracking as picking paint colors for the exterior. Indeed, the question of what shade to choose has always been a dilemma for the homeowner. Ready-mixed paints were first introduced in the mid-1800s, and with them came a desire to show off architectural features that were becoming common. By the second quarter of the 19th century, white walls with green shutters were ubiquitous, as Charles Dickens noted in a visit to Massachusetts in 1842: "All the buildings looked as if they had been painted that morning.... Every house is the whitest of white; every Venetian blind [shutter] is the greenest of green."

GET HELP FROM THE EXPERTS

As with interior paint, you can go the restorationist's route and employ a historical paint consultant to determine the home's original shades, or, failing that, which historically accurate hues might have been used on the house. If you just want to select colors that accentuate the best attributes of your house, many paint companies simplify choices with groupings of three or four hues that complement each other. Others go a step farther. Benjamin Moore, for instance, has software on its Web site that allows you to scan in a photograph of your house and then "try on" various color combinations.

FOLLOW COLOR PRINCIPLES

Remember that light advances, dark recedes. A home painted in light shades will appear larger and will seem closer to the front of the lot. The reverse is true. Deeper hues will create the impression that a home is set farther back, but they will also make a home look smaller. Consider as well the light in your climate and how the home will look in summer and winter. The diffused light of northern climes will intensify a bold color, and the strong light of warm climates will wash out a pale hue.

PAINT TO LAST

Once you've picked a color, follow these tips for an enduring paint job:

■ Paint often. Plan on redoing your house every five to eight years.

■ Recognize mildew. If your house looks discolored, put a dab of house-hold bleach on a spot. If the spot blanches, that means mildew, and it has to be scrubbed off before painting.

■ Let gutters and downspouts blend into the background by painting them the same hue as the siding rather than treating them as trim.

■ Solve moisture problems before you paint. If your gutters are bad or you have a roofing problem, the water will quickly ruin even the best paint job.

CONSIDER STAINING

Even though paint is the traditional finish for old houses, stains are not out of place. They particularly suit Colonial-style saltboxes and Capes, but can be used on just about any period home to good result. The advantage of stain is that because the pigment merely soaks into the grain of the wood (rather than binding to it), it won't peel or crack. It simply washes away over time. Stain is cheaper than paint and can last for up to 15 years when applied properly. However, because it is not as opaque as enamel, it will not cover up blemishes such as knots in old wood.

Saltbox Stakes
New Ground

A subdivision west of Chicago is one of the last places you'd expect to find a genuine-looking New England saltbox. But here it stands, its appearance belying both its setting and its newness. Back in the mid-1980s, a couple living in a big Illinois Victorian clipped an article about a reproduction saltbox. Marriage, work, and children kept them busy, but they never gave up their dream of owning such a house. Finally, when their children had flown the nest, they unfolded the clipping, purchased a lot in a subdivision, modified the design to fit their needs, and built. At 2,200 square feet their home is larger than the saltboxes of yesteryear, but its exterior appearance is fairly accurate, particularly in its complete lack of adornment. Saltboxes, which first appeared in New England in the mid- to late-1600s, got their name from the medieval salt boxes they closely resembled. Although often added to over time, they were historically simple dwellings, just as this house is. "Since we'd had the Victorian, we'd had enough fussy stuff," recalls the wife. "We loved the simplicity of the saltbox." It has taken their neighbors a while to get used to it, however. "At first they thought we were Amish," she recalls with a laugh. "Now they're just waiting for us to put the shutters up!"

For instant patina, the couple had the cedar clapboards on the house put on inside out, with the smooth back facing outwards and the rough front facing the framing. They then stained them a driftwood gray, which was absorbed by the clapboards in a mottled fashion. Because the subdivision required an attached garage, the pair made theirs look like a period addition. When their request for a plank front door with a thumb latch elicited a blank stare from their builder, they did the research themselves and provided him with a set of detailed instructions.

Clapboard and Shingle Siding

Up and down the East Coast for generations, clapboards and shingles were the preferred methods of covering homes, thanks to the large quantities of wood available. Today, 150-year-old buildings stand as a lasting testimony to wood siding's durability.

DECIDE ON THE SIDING

Shingles (which are vertical) usually give a home a more rustic appearance than clapboards (which are longer, horizontal strips of wood). Shingles are generally made of red or white cedar and, depending on how smooth they are, can be stained, painted, or left to weather on their own (cedar is a natural weather repellent). They come with different profiles. For a distinctive look, do a portion of the top of your house in fish-scale shingles and use clapboards on the bottom half. Or, if you have a Victorian or shingle-style house, create a relatively inexpensive accent with a circular or hexagonal design of shingles. Just be sure you approve a sample before the finished design is put up.

AVOID VINYL SIDING

Vinyl siding has many tempting attributes: It is inexpensive, doesn't rot, and the main part of your house will never need repainting. However, putting it up will mean permanently destroying the architectural integrity of your house and covering up original decorative details. Furthermore, vinyl siding can hide water damage until it becomes a major problem.

TRY FIBER CEMENT SIDING

Most old-house purists do not advocate the use of synthetic products on the exterior of houses, but many are singing the praises of fiber cement siding. It is a new material—made from portland cement, sand, cellulose, and other materials—that comes in 12-foot-long planks and many widths. It is offered in several wood-grain finishes, which means that you can repair a section of clapboards without the repair showing. Or, you can clad your entire house in this siding. It is impervious to termites and resists water damage; it also holds a paint finish much better than wood.

A Fresh Perspective

Yes, the Connecticut farmhouse was old—1870, to be exact; and yes, it had fabulous water views of Whalebone Creek, a tributary of the Connecticut River. But it had little in the way of personality when the architect acquired it in 1994. All distinguishing characteristics of the three-bedroom house had been stripped away by earlier generations. But what the house lacked, the setting more than made up for. "The changes I made were inspired by the site," the owner explains. "The place appealed to me because it was well situated, but essentially a blank canvas." He gutted the structure to the framing and opened up the floor plan to modernize it and take advantage of the water views. To give the house architectural presence, he added such classic Greek Revival elements as a two-story porch outfitted with railings and stately pilasters. Other period features included a pergola, a cedar-shake roof, and traditional six-over-six double-hung windows.

To give the facade of his 1870 farmhouse the appearance of an earlier Greek Revival dwelling, the architect-owner installed six-over-six windows and placed a decorative fanlight in the newly pedimented gable. Corner pilasters, typical of the era, complement the classic entablature around the front door. The granite walkway and the foundation are original to the house and were formed of stone quarried locally.

Rather than follow
the time-honored tradition of
putting the bigger, more
important rooms in the front
of the house, the owner put
the living room and the
master bedroom at the rear
(OPPOSITE). He also went
against expectations and
made the back of the home
the most elaborate so that it
would appear majestic from
the river. While most aspects
of the house's exterior are
fairly true to the Greek Revival
era, the large triangular
window in the gable was
designed by the owner. A
spacious attic the "size of a
ballroom" lies behind it.

Off the kitchen, a newly
built pergola (RIGHT) provides
a spot for summer dining.
Over time, the wisteria
climbing up the side will form
a living roof. The wrought-
iron table, a flea market find,
is topped with bluestone.

Roofing

In the past, roofs were made of slate, tile, metal, or wood shakes. Replacing a roof with one of these period options can be expensive, but they are probably the most durable options. Recently, manmade materials have been developed that mimic the appearance of these roofs at a fraction of the cost.

PICK THE COLOR CAREFULLY

To get an idea of the impact a roof has on the look of a dwelling, walk around your neighborhood. To select a color, look at how much of your roof shows from the street. If you see a lot of roof, then you may want to pick a high-profile shingle (a shingle that gives the appearance of a cedar shake, for instance), but if you see very little roof, then you should choose a shingle with a slimmer profile. Also take into consideration your climate. Some experts are recommending light-colored and even white roofs for homes in energy-starved California.

Think about your home's colors, including any brick or stone. Do you want the roof to become an accent or fade into the background? If your house has cool hues—blues, grays, or white—stick with cool roof colors such as black or gray. If your house has warm colors—brown, tan, taupe, yellow, or cream—stay with warm roof colors. For contrast, look at greens, blues, or reds. Get a sample of a few shingles and examine the flecks of different colors in each. If the shades on the shingles work up close then they will work farther away. But if they fight with your other colors, they aren't going to look right on the roof. Take a couple of strips of shingles and have your roofer put them on the roof. Step back and see which ones you like best. Choose with care. A roof is a big investment and not one you want to get tired of quickly.

HEAD TO TOWN HALL

Some areas have covenants that require homeowners to use a specific type of roofing—for instance, in parts of Baltimore, a slate roof must be replaced with another one of slate. Before you re-roof, check with your local building department.

Seaside Facelift

 ea air may be healthy for the body, but it wreaks havoc on a house's paint job. No sooner did the owners of this seaside Victorian (moved to New York's Long Island Sound 25 years ago) paint their home than it seemed it needed repainting. Traditional garb for a home of this ilk is painted clapboards and trim, but after their umpteenth paint job, the homeowners decided to clad the house in long-lasting cedar shingles instead. The solution made sense given the salty conditions, and was authentic for a turn-of-the-century home. The owners opted for white cedar over the more common western red cedar because pairing a Northeastern wood (white cedar) with a Northeastern house seemed more historically true. And since white cedar is a native wood, it should stand up well to the harsh weather conditions of the home's seaside location.

Durable clapboards (LEFT) now protect the house from salt and wind. Workers peeled off the original clapboards (RIGHT), then put on a layer of Tyvek house wrap as a moisture barrier and to provide insulation.

Before the renovation, peeling and flaking paint detracted from the charm of the small square windows (ABOVE LEFT) with vintage colored panes that were set on the diagonal. At the completion of the project, the same windows (ABOVE RIGHT), which illuminate and ventilate the interior of the Victorian's turret staircase, stand out against the crisp backdrop of the new shingles. The home's gingerbread trim had to be removed during the re-siding (OPPOSITE). Rotting sections were cut out and replaced with matching pieces. Only it and the window trim will need painting from now on. The shingles will gradually darken over time.

Exterior Trim

The earliest Colonial homes were bereft of many architectural niceties—they were too costly to produce, and considered unnecessary, to boot. But as wealth grew and craftsmen came to America, homeowners displayed their income with lavish hand-carved details on the interiors and exteriors of their houses. The trend began with the classical-inspired detailing on Georgian- and Federal-style buildings and reached its zenith with the fancy gingerbread details that adorned late 19th-century homes.

LOOK AROUND

Understanding the style of your house will help you decide what kind of trim to put on it. Put the wrong trim on a home and you will actually detract from its beauty and its value. Consult a professional. Look in books and at other houses to see what would look best on your dwelling.

MIND YOUR MATERIALS

If possible, invest in wood trim. Generally, it will look original to the house. Wood trim does require maintenance, however, in terms of regular scraping. You also shouldn't mix one species of wood with another. Different kinds of wood expand and contract at different rates, and may react differently to paints and stain.

   If you want elaborate details and can't afford wood, try polymer. It can be formed in intricate shapes and be painted. Another option for corner blocks and profiles that go around corners or curves is a new bendable molding. It makes details like arched window tops relatively inexpensive and easy to install.

CHOOSE CAREFULLY

As with the interior, millwork on the outside of a house can dress it up or evoke a completely different style. Don't go overboard. A few pieces of trim can carry a lot of visual weight.

DELIGHT IN DENTIL

Dentil molding along the soffit can quietly beautify a home. It gracefully formalizes the home without over-whelming the architecture.

CROWN THE WINDOWS

Embellish windows inexpensively with a piece of crown molding above the header of each window. One architect advocates this technique only for the bottom windows, leaving the upper ones unadorned to create a hierarchy. When ordering your windows, verify what kind of trim is included. Often, for a nominal charge, you can obtain a wider casing that will have a more gracious appearance.

ADORN THE DOOR

Add importance to the front door with a pediment or fan light with molding and a keystone.

Windows and Doors

Nothing affects the appearance of a house as much as its windows and front door. When undertaking any exterior renovation, buy the best windows and doors you can afford. The money will be well spent.

KEEP IN BALANCE

Symmetry and balance are important: Line any new windows up with existing ones. Most preservation guidelines call for retaining all existing window openings on the "public" sides of a house. Use specialty windows—elliptical, arched, round—with care. They are a good way to dress up a plain 20th-century Colonial revival but are often misused. Forego Palladian windows—they've been grossly overused—unless you have a grand home that can carry such an architectural statement.

If you are enlarging the windows, make them taller instead of wider; the proportions will be better. When windows were made bigger in the past, they were always taller—widening them would have required cutting the studs.

CHOOSE THE BEST

The front door is a good opportunity to put decorative glass on a house and add greatly to its overall impact. If at all possible, spend extra on a custom solid-wood front door. It will last longer, add value to your house, and look more beautiful and appropriate than stock doors made of steel (the cheapest option) or wood-veneer doors that have an engineered wood core (a low-cost alternative to solid wood). When door shopping, look for crisp lines. In general, the finer the detailing, the better the door.

In lieu of traditional French doors, consider the new sliding French doors. They look just like the classic models, but they slide, eliminating the need for floor clearance to open the door; in addition they are more weather tight.

Inspecting an Old House

BY THEIR NATURE, OLD HOUSES INSPIRE *well-deserved romantic notions. But the romance of owning an old house should not blind you to its realities—that wood porch may look beautiful, but its foundation may need to be completely rebuilt.*

Soft or squishy floorboards could indicate a problem with the foundation. At the same time, of course, you may discover some pleasant surprises—an old wideboard floor found under a protective layer of cheap linoleum, for example.

So, before you consider buying an old house with all its idiosyncrasies, you should thoroughly inspect the property, looking for evidence of problems or damage on the surface and behind the scenes. Once you understand the house better, you can more accurately evaluate whether the property is right for you. It's important not to take on too much—physically, emotionally, or financially. But, equally, don't eliminate a house simply because it calls for repair. Every old house needs work of some kind.

The house inspection process described here is no substitute for a full inspection by a certified home inspector. If you become serious about a particular house, you should invest in professional advice before making a commitment.

Tools

Take along a flashlight, tape measure, binoculars, awl, and notebook to the house. The binoculars will allow you to examine areas such as the chimney and roof. The awl (a pointed metal shank attached to a wood or plastic handle) is for poking into wood or mortar to test for deterioration. You should bring a paper mask and gloves, as it is not uncommon to encounter rodent droppings in basements and attics of old buildings. And be sure to wear shoes with sturdy soles to protect your feet from nails and debris.

Record your thoughts and observations in the notebook and, if you can, use a still or video camera to photograph large areas of the house as well as details. Not only will the images refresh your memory after you've left the site, but they will also become a valuable record should you purchase the home.

The Exterior

You can learn quite a lot about an old building just by walking around and studying its exterior. Because moisture is the single biggest enemy of an old house, much of your exterior inspection will involve looking for evidence of weather-

and water-tightness. If you note a problem and can guess its cause (broken gutters that have caused water damage to trimwork, for example), write it down.

Walls

Square and plumb walls signal structural soundness. But because all houses shift and settle over time, older structures rarely have walls that are square and plumb. Old houses are only as sound as the original work, and even the soundest construction will deteriorate if it's not maintained properly.

Minor variations from perfectly square can usually be fixed with repairs to the framing. If a wall is conspicuously distorted, however, it could point to a problem with the home's foundation, an area where repairs are labor-intensive and expensive. If you suspect a foundation problem, you should have the structure examined professionally.

Old House Basics: Framing

Nearly all houses in America—even brick houses—use wood to support the roof and the floors. But the style of wood framing has changed over the years. Until the early 19th century, builders laboriously hand-crafted wood frames from massive timbers held together by interlocking joints. This type of structure, which is experiencing a resurgence in custom home construction, is called **timber-frame** or **post-and-beam building**.

The use of **stick-built frames**—frames constructed from standardized dimensioned lumber, such as 2x4s—began to gain popularity between 1830 and 1850, after the widespread use of the circular saw made the production of dimensioned lumber available. It is extremely rare to find hand-hewn timbers in houses built after 1875. Accompanying this shift was the change from handmade to manufactured nails and other fasteners.

WHAT TO LOOK FOR:

■ **Tilting wall.** If a whole wall is tilted toward one end or the other, it may mean that the foundation has sunk or is sinking.

■ **Leaning wall.** If the wall isn't plumb, structural timbers may be damaged, missing, or undersized, allowing the wall to move.

■ **Splayed wall.** If a wall splays outward at the top, it probably indicates missing roof components.

■ **Bowed wall, out or in.** This is probably due to damaged or missing structural components. Major bulges may signal trouble in the foundation or inside the walls.

SIDING

Note the material of any exterior siding. If the original siding has been covered by vinyl or aluminum, it may be hiding a lot of problems. If asbestos siding is badly damaged, this will need to be removed by a professional. This may be expensive.

Blistering, flaking, or peeling paint on wood clapboards or shingles signals the migration of water vapor from the interior of the house to the exterior. In time, the moisture inside the wall will rot the framing. Unfortunately, the culprit in many such cases is insulation. Although insulation is a standard weatherization treatment, it can actually trap moisture within the wall. Installing

Old House Basics: Siding

In the same way that the development of circular sawblades radically changed house framing, it also changed **exterior siding**. **Clapboards** manufactured after about 1830, for example, are typically longer than the four-foot to six-foot lengths produced previously. **Shingles** made in the 18th century were split out of wood and rather thick; they're actually called **"shakes"** today to distinguish them from sawn shingles. Evolving technology also had an effect on sawn shingles, as they were produced in a variety of fancy shapes by the mid-19th century. If you're looking at a **brick** house, try to discern if the bricks look identical and uniform or if they look handmade. You probably won't find machine-made bricks before the 1850s unless they were installed as part of a repair.

some type of vapor barrier or vapor retardant is one way to remedy this problem, but you should consult an expert to decide what would work best for your house.

The ideal clapboard or shingle is smooth, whole, and without punky or spongy areas. Clapboards or shingles that are badly warped, split, or rotted must be replaced, especially if you can see the sheathing underneath. Bear in mind that it can be difficult to patch-repair siding, since removing one area often damages adjacent areas. What

initially looks like a simple job can quickly become expensive.

If the home you're evaluating is brick, look for horizontal cracks—they're generally more important than vertical ones because they indicate settling. Pay particular attention to the mortar joints. Since repairing deteriorating mortar joints is a big, expensive project (they have to be raked, cleaned, and repointed), poke around with your awl to test for crumbling. Brick doesn't betray water problems as obviously as wood, but bulges in the brickwork

are a tip-off that a water problem has damaged the interior wood framing. As with wood siding, don't be fooled by a glossy new paint job. There may be problems lurking underneath.

Windows and Doors

Record the number of windows and doors in your notebook. If you notice that many are rotted, remember these can be expensive to replace, especially if they are not standard sizes. (Window sizes did not become standard until about the mid-19th century.) Standard-size units will be much less costly than custom-ordered products.

WHAT TO LOOK FOR:

▪ **Sticky or jammed windows and doors.** This could indicate settling either in the past or ongoing. Windows and doors should fit snugly.

▪ **Rotted window and door framing.** Pay particular attention to the corner joints, where water may have penetrated the end grain of the wood, and all the little pockets where water can settle and cause rot. Use your awl and flashlight to test for punky, sodden wood.

▪ **Damaged or absent flashing above doors and windows.** Suspect water damage, and make a note to also check the wall sheathing and framing underneath for signs of water damage that could be expensive to repair.

■ **Water damage on windowsills and thresholds.** These wear-prone areas are susceptible to major damage, especially if the wood has been left unpainted. These areas should be in good repair and sloped to shed water.

■ **Cracked glazing.** You should expect a certain amount of damage to glass in an uninhabited building, but excessive cracking may indicate that the house was or is settling.

■ **Any voids in the glazing putty.** Putty should look whole, to stop water from seeping into the wood.

■ **Exterior doors that don't fit snugly or are not weatherproof.** If they are made of hardwood they may be worth repairing and restoring.

■ **The existence of storm windows.** Replacing several custom-sized wood storm windows can be extremely expensive.

The Roof

Use your binoculars to check the roofline. Ideally, the roof should be straight at the ridge and eaves. A sagging, waving, or uneven roof could be the result of missing or rotted timbers, foundation settlement, or poor original construction. (Your examination of the attic later on will provide even more information about the condition of the roof.) Water stains visible under the eaves may indicate that water is getting through the roof and running down the rafters.

Old House Basics: Roofing

In early American house-building, **shakes** and **shingles** for roofing were identical to those used for exterior siding, except they were usually cut longer—36 inches compared with 18 to 24 inches. In houses dating later than 1900, you may find asphalt shingles as well as wood. **Sheet tin roofing**, which came in large rolls, was usually found on the homes of wealthy city dwellers after the beginning of the 19th century, but didn't become common in outlying areas until the middle of the century. The use of slate, an extremely cumbersome material to transport, became more widespread as railroads multiplied around the time of the Civil War.

Check the roofing material. Shingles should be fairly evenly spaced; if they're not, the installation was probably not professional. Damaged asphalt shingles will show curly or torn edges. If wood shingles have splits or breaks and look punky or if you see moss, there's water damage, which may have seeped into the sheathing and even the framing below. If you see more than one layer of shingles at the edge of the roof, you may have to strip the roof before you can safely lay new shingles atop. This is not necessarily a major job, but it is more costly than installing new shingles above the old. Also, be on the lookout for water damage that may have occurred before the roof was shingled over. If the roof shows signs of recent repair (you can easily pick patches out because the new shingles won't match the color of the old ones), remember to take a closer look at this from the attic.

Slate roofs are costly but extremely durable. Even if a slate roof has a few missing or broken pieces, it may not be a major undertaking to replace them (although you will have to check in the attic to see if water has leaked through to damage the underlying structure). Look for large areas of damage, which may have been caused by the house shifting (or a fallen tree). Unattractive rusty streaks on the roof indicate that the nails used weren't galvanized. This means that they will eventually corrode and may, over many years, compromise the structural integrity of the roof. Reinstalling an entire slate roof, or replacing all the fasteners, is very expensive, so this is something you should keep a close eye on.

Metal roofs are also costly to replace, but if the structure is sound, they can be refurbished with an application of special roof coating. The trouble areas on metal roofs are usually found at the seams, where water can penetrate. Remember to note down any roof problems so that you can check these same problems during your attic inspection.

FLASHING

You can tell if flashing is damaged because it will be pitted with rust and may show signs of patching. This is a concern because it may indicate water damage to the wood structure underneath. Small pockets of rust here or there are not an issue, since they can be sanded off. But pay special attention to valley flashing (angled flashing, for example at the joint between the main roof and a dormer roof) and the flashing around chimneys and stacks. Make

sure these areas are in fact flashed, and then look for damage as described above. If the house does not have metal drip edges installed under the last row of shingles, be sure to check for water damage on—and in—interior walls.

GUTTERS

The gutters should look solid and be attached securely to the house with brackets. If the gutters are filled with debris and look like they haven't been cleaned out for a long time, there may be water damage at the roof or foundation level. Wooden gutters, which are usually nailed to the trim, tend to go soft on the trim side with age. Use your awl to detect spongy, rotted wood. If the wood gutter system is part of the cornice treatment, you may not be able to replace them with metal gutters without also going to the expense of replacing the cornices.

The Foundation

Because foundation work can be expensive, a sound foundation is often the difference between a house that's financially viable and one that is not. Any problems with a foundation must be solved before other renovation work takes place. If you have any doubts, hire an engineer to look at the foundation.

As with the exterior walls, you should look for signs of twisting, leaning, or waviness in foundation walls. Fieldstone foundations are often difficult to evaluate, since the stones are irregular and rarely line up in nice even planes. Regardless of the material you find, record mortar condition, cracks, and deterioration. As a general rule of thumb, a crack that's $\frac{1}{8}$ inch wide or larger is considered serious, because it may mean that the foundation (or another part of the house) is shifting. Mortar patches or caulked and painted foundations may be cover-ups for serious problems. Use your awl to probe any area that looks suspicious.

SETTLING

Settling is one of the most common foundation problems. Because the walls of the house are attached to the foundation, when a section of foundation sinks, so does whatever it's attached to. To compound the problem, the redistribution of forces caused by the shifted framework will place new stresses on the rest of the house, often causing a domino effect as the house begins to pull apart.

Minor settling is to be expected in any old house and can usually be repaired fairly easily. Severe settling is a far more serious matter, and needs expert consultation. You should contact a professional if you can't tell the difference.

During your exterior inspection, note the slope of the yard around the house. Ground sloping away from the house will help water drain, while ground that slopes toward the house will funnel water right where it is likely to cause damage. Poorly maintained window wells and cellar entries can also channel enough water into a basement or crawl space to destroy a foundation and should be repaired immediately.

SILLS

Sill beams (heavy timbers between the top of the foundation and the house framing) are prone to water damage and rot because of their proximity to the ground. If a sill rots out, it can have the same effect as a settling foundation, pulling the house wall downward. While you can't see the sills from outside the building, if the lower rows of siding are severely damaged, it is likely that the sheathing and sills are, too. As with most old-house problems, it is hard to generalize, but if the damage is severe enough it may not be cost-effective to make repairs.

Chimneys

You can't do a thorough inspection of the chimney from ground level,
even with binoculars, but you can pick up on obvious damage such as loose or missing bricks and bulges.

WHAT TO LOOK FOR:

■ **Cracks in the masonry.** As with a brick wall, horizontal cracks are usually more serious than vertical ones, since they point to settling of the house.

■ **Missing chunks of mortar.** This may indicate that the structure of the chimney has been compromised.

■ **A cracked flue.** This may let hot gasses escape, which could ignite wood framing members in the attic. As a rule of thumb, the flue should protrude about an inch above the cap. (If there's no flue, as in some Victorian houses where the fireplace was for decoration only, you can't burn wood in a fireplace or wood stove for safety reasons.)

■ **Unaligned flue tiles.** Check for this by looking down into the chimney. If tiles are not aligned, you may need to reline the chimney, which can be a very expensive project.

■ **Lack of or damaged chimney cap.** This can lead to interior water damage, which you may notice during your attic inspection.

■ **Unsound chimney flashing.** Water damage due to missing or damaged flashing can be severe enough to require a new roof.

■ **Weak chimney support.** Check inside the house to ensure that each chimney is supported on its own footing and not resting on the floor.

The Interior

For the able sleuth, an old home can be a source of fascinating information about the lives and tastes of prior inhabitants. Many are the stories told about ripping out a "modern" closet or wall to find traces, called "witness marks," of what used to exist beneath. Period paint colors and wallcoverings, antique moldings, even old letters or memorabilia may be discovered during interior refurbishment.

Whether or not you choose to renovate the house to its original appearance using the clues you find, it's always enlightening to find out as much as you can about an old house before you finalize your decorating plans. Likewise, it's wise to identify features of architectural character and importance that should be preserved. Old homes often contain exquisite decorative details such as wainscoting and other woodwork, and even if they're in poor shape now they may deserve to be sensitively restored.

The Basement

As a rule of thumb, the newer the home, the more basement you'll probably find. This makes perfect sense when you remember that our Colonial ancestors didn't have backhoes at their disposal. Building even a modest basement was an arduous, back-breaking task.

If you are inspecting a house that has a basement, it can be a source of important information. In fact, the condition of this area will probably tell you whether your dreams of owning an old house are likely to contain the seeds of nightmares.

Begin your survey with the basement stairs, which, often neglected by homeowners, can be wobbly and unsafe. But take heart. Repairing, or even replacing, basement stairs is not an expensive or difficult task.

Inspect the foundation walls. You're looking for many of the same conditions you checked for on the exterior: no serious cracks (which could point at settling), plumb walls, solid mortar (if the foundation is brick or mortared stone), and an overall solid structure. Open all the basement doors, and if their fit is tight, suspect that settling may be the culprit. A musty smell, water stains, and whitish mineral deposits (called efflorescence) on walls are all indications of water problems.

Note the material and condition of the basement floor, and look for evidence of water there, as well. Water usually leaves clues that can be read even during dry months. On concrete floors water will leave stains or dark blotches. If you notice an exceptionally clean stone floor, or a particularly smooth dirt floor, suspect persistent flooding and not meticulous housekeeping. Peek under the bottom of fixtures such as oil burners to see if any rust is visible. Check for water marks on the bottom of the basement framing. This can indicate that the house may experience seasonal flooding—in the spring, for example, when ground water is high. Remember that although localized water problems may be fixable, more serious issues in a basement are rarely easily cured, the claims of miracle barrier products to the contrary.

If you've ruled out problems with the foundation and water, it's probably safe to say that most of what you'll find in the basement is repairable. Don't neglect to inspect the sills from the inside, however, since, as discussed previously, their closeness to masonry and water makes them prone to rot. Prod suspicious areas, especially on the bottom of the sill, with your awl, and look for dark streaks on the wood—a sign of dry rot, which is caused by fungal infestation. Make sure that all wood posts have a good footing for support.

One last note: If the sills are covered by a wall that runs up to

Old House Basics: Foundations

The earliest American houses rested on **wood foundations**. It didn't take long, however, for settlers to discover that wood was far too vulnerable to water and insects to be durable. **Fieldstone** thus became the material of choice in most of the colonies, since stone was all too plentiful from clearing the land. Sometimes it was laid dry, sometimes with mortar. **Mortared brick** was more widely used in other parts of the country, where stone wasn't abundant. **Concrete** (both poured and block) didn't enjoy widespread use until the 20th century.

the floorboards of the first floor, you probably haven't been looking at the inside of the real foundation wall. Often a wall is added to the inside of the foundation for cosmetic purposes. Remember that these walls do nothing to support a house structurally, so you should try to get access to the foundation wall underneath for a thorough inspection.

Floors

Uneven flooring is hard to miss and not uncommon in old houses. You can often see bulges and dips or feel them as you walk around. Rolling a marble will give you a sense of the slope of the floors. Often, floors can move, distort, or squeak when the structure supporting them shifts or provides poor support. This problem may be caused by undersized joists, or by inadequate (or nonexistent) bracing between joists. (Work conducted by the previous homeowners over the years can also compromise the integrity of beams and joists.) Weak structural components may also be the result of wet conditions that have allowed rot or insects to thrive. Typically, floor problems aren't that hard to fix, providing the rest of the house is structurally sound. Sometimes all that's required is joist reinforcement and shimming.

Note the floor finish in your notebook. You may discover anything from layers of wood, paint, and linoleum to gleaming restored wide boards cut from old-growth softwood trees. (In houses built before the 1800s, you're not likely to find fancy finishes, such as stenciling, since it was still common practice to treat the floor to a hard daily scrub with water and soap or sand.)

Walls

Record the overall condition of the walls in each room of the house. Focus on the corners, where walls meet, because these areas usually

---

Insects and Old Houses

With any luck you'll find a slice of metal between the top of the foundation and the wooden sill of your house. This is called a termite shield, and is designed to keep bugs out of the woodwork.

Termites are the greatest insect threat to wood houses. If you find hard earthen tubes on the foundation, it is a sure sign of termite activity. (Termites avoid all contact with fresh air and invade the house through a network of tubes, although in warmer areas they may forego tubes and nest directly in the wood.) Little piles of partially digested wood also indicate termite activity.

Carpenter ants can sometimes be just as destructive as termites. Like termites, they favor moist environments, so anywhere there's water damage is a potential point of infestation. These insects are quite visible as they parade in and out of the house along established trails; you can also detect their presence by the piles of coarse sawdust they leave behind.

Fine powdery sawdust and tiny holes in posts and beams may be signs of **wood-boring beetles**. For any assessment or treatment of insect activity, consult a professional exterminator.

show stress first. Cracks in the ceiling may indicate that the walls are moving on a shifting foundation. Peer into the closets. Damage marks there may not have been repaired, and can give good testimony about structural or moisture problems the house has suffered in the past.

Depending on the overall age of the house, the interior walls may be finished with various materials—from wood planks to plaster. Check plaster walls for major cracks and bulges, since these may indicate the house was or is settling and needs structural shoring. (Hairline cracks are common with plaster finishes and are easily repaired.) Lean on plaster walls to make sure they're sturdy. If you notice excessive flaking or peeling, suspect a moisture problem. (This will be most visible on ceilings under bathrooms.)

Review the condition of paint throughout the house. Old paint contains lead, and exposed lead paint should always be removed with chemical removers (not sanded) or covered up, especially if you have children. In bathrooms, check tile and grout lines for soundness. Spongy areas of the wall can often indicate rotted framing behind it.

Sometimes you'll be lucky and find evidence of old paints and wallpapers that had been covered up by past remodelers. These finishes can help you determine the function and tone of a room, and can aid your efforts should you decide to restore a period feel to the house.

Lastly, before leaving each room, note the number of electrical outlets there, and make an estimate of the number you'll need.

The Attic

Like the basement, the attic is an overlooked area that nevertheless can provide you with a lot of useful information. It may also very well be a treasure trove of leftover building materials and other objects. And it is here that you should try to confirm any suspicions raised during your study of the roof and chimney.

Note whether you can see daylight through the roof of the attic *before* you turn on your flashlight. If you can, you'll definitely find water damage at those points.

Check the rafters. Any sagging indicates they are not strong enough to support the roof weight. Look for other problems—signs of leaks, water damage, fungal growth, insect infestation, or cracking. Try following water stains to their conclusion, and use your awl to look for rot.

Inspect the sheathing (or roof boards) under the roofing material. Small areas of damage can be patched. Check that there's a vent at each end of the attic to allow air circulation. If it is absent or blocked, look for damage from condensation or insects. Make a note of the type of insulation, if any, and its thickness. The insulation should be dry.

Lastly, check the brick and the mortar of the chimney. If there is a smell of creosote, it could indicate a problem with the chimney flue.

Mechanical Systems

Old houses do not have the modern conveniences that are now common in many new homes. Not everyone needs a trash compactor or central air conditioning, but old structures can be remarkably unaccommodating to modern innovations; adding them can be a surprisingly expensive element in your overall budget.

The Electrical System

It is likely that your electrical system will need to be upgraded—an expensive proposition. The hub of the electrical system is in the basement. You will probably find either a gray service-entry panel box or a fuse box and a tangle of electrical "improvements" that have been added over time. Check either one for the maximum service rating, which is usually stated on the main breaker or fuse block. If the service is less than 100 amps, you're below the minimum required for today's lifestyles and the system will need updating. If you have high electrical needs, such as several computers, you'll need 200-amp service.

Under no circumstances should you touch electrical components yourself. If you're interested in the house, call in an electrician for a consultation. Ask about the type of electrical cable that is installed and its overall condition (you can get some idea of this from the basement, where, if you look up, you'll see wires running along the joists—check for fraying and cracks). Also ask about the number of circuits that feed the house, and whether adding a subpanel would make sense. Ask if the house has been rewired, and, if so, if it conforms to local building code. There will undoubtedly be other work required to bring a house up to code, such as installing GFCIs (ground-fault circuit inter-rupters) in bathrooms and kitchens.

You can get some sense of the magnitude and cost of the electrical work needed from what you've already noted in the house—it's difficult, for example, to add circuits and outlets in a home with plaster walls. Timber-frame homes can also pose a challenge because structural components may have to be cut to install new wiring. Products such as track wiring with movable outlets can help avoid such costly proce-dures. This type of wiring wraps around the wall at baseboard height —if you have ornate baseboards, you can even conceal the wire in the molding. You should ask an electrician if there are other non-invasive alternatives available.

The Plumbing System

It's hard to evaluate a plumbing system for the same reason it can be difficult to update one—almost all the plumbing is hidden within walls and ceilings. As with the electrical system, if you're serious about the house, talk to an expert, in this case a licensed plumber, before buying. But there are some observations you can easily make on your own.

Check the bathrooms to ensure that fixtures—toilets, bathtubs, sinks, and showers—are sitting securely on the floor, that there is no evidence of leakage, and that they flush well. If the toilet gurgles when you drain a sinkful of water, the system may have venting flaws.

It is also important to note where fresh water comes from. If it comes from a well, ask when the well was drilled and how much water it supplies. It is always a good idea to get the water tested.

If there is a septic system, walk the septic fields, watching for spongy ground and waste smells, which would indicate that the system needs work. If there is natu-ral gas service, use your nose to alert you to leaks, and your eyes to judge the overall condition of the lines. If you have any doubt, call the gas company for an inspection.

WHAT TO LOOK FOR:

■ **Poor water pressure.** Turn on the cold water in the bathroom on the top floor and simultaneously flush the toilets and see if the water pressure is affected. Poor pressure can be caused by undersized pipes or sediment deposits in the pipes. Either way, you may have a problem.

■ **Water hammer.** Turn a faucet on and quickly shut it off. If you hear a hammering sound, the supply lines may have to be accessed for repair.

■ **Corroded supply pipes.** Galvanized iron supply pipes, which corrode over time and have a useful life of about 25 years, may need to be replaced with modern copper pipes.

■ **An old water heater.** Open the drain valve at the base of the heater and check if the water is clear or if it pours forth rust and scale— an indication of age.

The Heating System

This is usually a very difficult area for laypeople to inspect, so much like the plumbing system, if you're seriously thinking of investing in an old house, bring in a professional for a thorough inspection. But there is some information you can easily gather on your own.

Find out the age of the furnace. Generally, older furnaces are less efficient and are therefore usually worth replacing. Ask the current homeowner for recent heating bills. You should also turn up the thermostat to see how quickly the radiators warm up or air comes through the ducts. Other areas of concern include safety, the projected useful life of the current heating system, and energy efficiency.

Three Philosophies of Home Improvement

There are three approaches to fixing up older houses. **Preservation** is the philosophy that old homes should be preserved as educational tools for future generations. The word "old" has different definitions: Some preservationists include only houses built before 1850, while others believe that newer homes should also be included under the **preservation umbrella**. In practical terms, preservationists believe that it is society's obligation to conserve the original character and construction of older homes. This means that a **preservationist** might paint over existing paint, but probably would not remove the underlying layers. If serious repairs were needed, they would be carefully documented through notes, drawings, and still or video photography. This philosophy is slightly different from **restoration** (a branch of preservation), which asks that a home be painstakingly restored to the way it existed during a particular period of time.

The second approach, **renovation** (sometimes called **rehabilitation**), is the practice of refurbishing an old house to satisfy modern needs while retaining the best period features of the house and remaining true to its style. Modern materials are used as necessary: manufactured wood, latex paint, polyurethane, double-glazed windows, and so on, but the work is handled with a sensitivity to the house's original architecture.

Remodeling is the third and final approach. It has taken on a bad reputation over the years, as insensitive tradesmen continue to destroy the architectural significance of old structures. The main focus of remodeling is typically convenience and cost-effectiveness, which can often wreak havoc on the character of an old house. Still, if a house has been "improved" over the years—until it's no longer recognizable as any one style—there's probably no historical harm in a well-done remodeling job.

Architects and Contractors

THE PROFESSIONALS YOU CHOOSE *to work on your old home will reflect your desire to preserve, renovate, or remodel. There are different philosophies associated with each activity, as described on page 179. Depending on the route you follow, you may*

work with one or several professionals, including architects, contractors, subcontractors, expert tradespeople, and specialists in various fields, such as an architectural historian or historic finishes analyst.

Selecting an Architect

To begin, you may choose to work with an architect or a designer, the difference being that an architect is certified and licensed and a designer is not. Either professional can help target problems, suggest design possibilities, and help select appropriate materials for the job, but only an architect can provide stamped working drawings, which are required by most municipalities to issue building permits. If you are coping with structural problems, you'll need either an architect's or engineer's expertise anyway, so it might make financial sense to take advantage of the architect's design training at the beginning of the project.

The extent of your relationship with an architect depends on the work to be done. You may retain an architect either to consult during certain parts of the job, to enlarge a kitchen or knock out a back wall, for example, or to oversee the entire job. If all you need are working drawings, the architect will probably bill on an hourly basis. For new construction, architects often receive payment calculated as a percentage of the entire project; but because there are so many unknowns with old houses, architects usually prefer to work to a fixed fee plus expenses.

Choose an architect who is sensitive to the needs of old buildings. If the home is in a historic neighborhood, ask neighbors for references. Otherwise, you can check with State Historic Preservation Officers, local historical societies, or landmarks preservation groups for recommendations. You can also contact your local chapter of the AIA (American Institute of Architects) for referrals, or scan the classified sections of magazines dedicated to preservation and renovation. Always check the architect's resume for evidence of successful management of preservation or renovation projects that are on the scale of your house. (An extra benefit of contracting an architect experienced with old homes is that he or she is likely to have a network of knowledgeable contractors and subcontractors.) Call the references provided and, if you can, visit the completed buildings.

The architect will undoubtedly want to pay a visit to the site before submitting a written proposal and work schedule. If you'll be retaining the architect for drawings only, expect to pay for this visit—and any consultations—on an hourly basis. Otherwise, the architect will probably include the initial work as part of the larger package.

Selecting a Contractor

With any luck, a good contractor will fall into your lap thanks to your architect's recommendations. If you don't plan to work with an architect, you'll have to find the general contractor on your own. Once again, ask around the neighborhood for recommendations; local banks usually have a good sense of reliable businesspeople in the area. A call to the Better Business Bureau will tell you if any complaints have been lodged against the professionals you're considering. General contractors should be licensed, and they are responsible for checking the licenses and insurance coverage of the subcontractors to make sure state requirements are met.

Once you have the names of several contractors, schedule initial interviews, at the site if possible. Try to get a feeling for the contractor's technical expertise, sensitivity to old homes, overall integrity, personality, and ability to communicate. Give each contractor a set of written specifications and ask for a competitive proposal in writing. These proposals should break out materials and time separately, so you can better evaluate what you're buying. Ask for a commitment to a schedule, too—and get this in writing also. Work on old houses is always full of surprises that involve extra time and money, so you can safely assume that any dates will be approximate!

Don't feel obliged to snap up the lowest bid, since it may also reflect the lowest quality materials. Some homeowners make it a point, all things being equal, to throw out the top and bottom bids and take the one in the middle.

Homeowner as Contractor

Many people act as their own contractors with superb results, but this is not a role that suits everyone. Before you decide to tackle this job yourself, make sure you know all that it involves. Without a contractor, the job of hiring subcontractors falls to you, and it can be difficult to find tradespeople knowledgeable in preservation and renovation, since this work comprises a small portion of the construction business. If the job is associated with a union, such as plastering or masonry, you can ask for union references, or you can check classified ads in preservation and renovation magazines. Always check the references of anyone you hire, and ask to visit jobs in progress. Keep in mind, however, that if you don't have experience in construction, it can be extremely difficult to judge the quality or efficiency of subcontractors' work.

Some other issues you must deal with as a contractor include setting schedules, verifying workers' hours, ordering materials, and meeting with inspectors—just to name a few. Obviously, the more complex your project, the more involved the job of general contractor becomes. But even for a relatively small project you must be extremely well organized and visit the job site as needed.

If you do decide that you have the resources, the time, and most of all the desire to act as your own contractor, be sure to purchase one of the many valuable books available on the subject: An investment in your education up front can save thousands of dollars later.

Resources

Associations

The Association for Preservation Technology International (APT)
4513 Lincoln Ave., Suite 213
Lisle, IL 60532-1290 USA
(888) 723-4242
www.apti.org
Dedicated to the use of technology for the conservation of historic buildings and districts.

Advisory Council on Historic Preservation
1100 Pennsylvania Avenue NW, Suite 809
Old Post Office Building
Washington, DC 20004
(202) 606-8503
www.achp.gov
State Historic Preservation Officers administer the national historic preservation program at the state level and offer useful advice on home restoration issues. You can receive a list of state officers by writing to the above address or consulting their Web site.

National Conference of State Historic Preservation Officers
Suite 342 Hall of the States
444 North Capitol Street, NW
Washington, DC 20001-7572
(202) 624-5465
www.ncshpo.org

National Park Service
1849 C Street NW
Washington, DC 20240
(202) 208-6843
www.nps.gov
Publishes "Preservation Briefs" (also available on the Website), which offer easy-to-read guidance on preserving and restoring historic buildings.

National Trust for Historic Preservation
1785 Massachusetts Ave., NW
Washington, DC 20036-2117
(202) 588-6000
Offers advice on the restoration and preservation of historic homes and buildings. Also offers a Historic Homeowner's Bookstore online.

Websites

www.countryliving.com
For inspiration and additional resources.

www.loghomes.com
Offers links to builders, mills, manufacturers, and other companies that specialize in log home construction and maintenance.

www.oldhouse.com
Dedicated to the preservation and enjoyment of old houses and historical buildings.

www.oldhousejournal.com
The Old House Journal magazine's Web site. Includes sections on old house products, historic house plans, professional directories, and general tips and advice.

www.oldhouseweb.net
Dedicated to old house enthusiasts; offers how-to stories, features, general advice on restorations, and an online book and video store.

www.Remodelingweb.com
A home improvement and do-it-yourself site. Offers stories, directories, advice, and links to many related Web sites.

www.taunton.com/fh
Fine Homebuilding's online magazine. Offers practical advice on home building for both the new- and old-home owner.

www.thisoldhouse.com/toh/
Offers advice on improving your old or your new home.

Architectural Salvage

Architectural Accents
2711 Piedmont Road
Atlanta, GA 30305
(404) 266-8700
Old and reproduction architectural elements.

Architectural Antiques
Downtown Minneapolis
1330 Quincy St. NE
Minneapols, MN. 55413
612.332.8344
www.archantiques.com
Architectural salvage and reproductions.

Architectural Antique Warehouse
17985 Highway 27
Fairhope, Alabama 36532
(251) 928-2880
www.architectural-antiques.com
Architectural salvage including doors, hardware, stained and beveled glass, mantels, gates, and ornamental iron.

Architectural Bank
1824 Felicity Street
New Orleans, LA
(504) 523-2702
Old and reproduction shutters, mantels, and hardware.

Architectural Emporium
207 Adams Avenue
Canonsburg, PA 15317
(724) 746-4301
www.architectural-emporium.com
Restored antique chandeliers, light fixtures, wall sconces, mantels, doors, newel posts, and vintage plumbing.

Architectural Salvage, Inc.
3 Mill Street
Exeter, NH 03833
(603) 773-5635
www.oldhousesalvage.com
Lighting fixtures, bath fixtures, hardware, mantels, doors, windows, flooring, doorknobs, stair parts, floor registers, and ironwork.

Architectural Savage Warehouse
53 Main Street
Burlington, VT 05401
(802) 658-5011
www.greatsalvage.com
Salvaged architectural antiques and fixtures including mantels, doors, windows, hardware, plumbing, lighting, columns, and posts.

By-Gone Days Antiques
114P Freeland Lane
Charlotte, NC 28217
(704) 527-8718
Door hardware, doors, mantels, and many other unusual and rare pieces.

Carolina Architectural Salvage
110 South Palmer Street
Ridgeway, SC 29130
(803) 337-3939
www.cogansantiques.com
Architectural items including light fixtures, mantels, stained glass, exterior and interior doors, hardware, plumbing fixtures, and ironwork.

The Emporium
1800 Westheimer
Houston, TX 77098
(713) 528-3808
www.the-emporium.com
Salvage and reproduction elements, including stained and beveled glass, fluted columns, and clawfoot bathtubs.

First Period Colonial Preservation/Restoration
P.O. Box 31
Kingston, NH 03848
(603) 642-8613
www.firstperiodcolonial.com
Preservation and restoration of structural and decorative elements in 17th-, 18th-, and 19th-century New England buildings. Re-creation of moldings, doors, windows, and paneling.

Gargoyles
512 Third Street
Philadelphia, PA 19147
(215) 629-1700
Decorative and architectural house elements.

Historic Tile Company
4524 Brazil Street
Los Angeles, CA 90039
(818) 547-4247
www.historictile.com
Antique stones, bricks, and roof tiles imported from Europe.

Irreplaceable Artifacts
14 Second Avenue
New York, NY 10003
(212) 777-2900
www.irreplaceableartifacts.com
Interior and exterior architectural elements from New York City and its surroundings.

Ohmega Salvage
2407 San Pablo Avenue
Berkeley, CA 94702
(510) 204-0767
www.ohmegasalvage.com
Architectural details including antique plumbing fixtures, tubs, sinks, hardware, old wrought iron, doors, and windows.

Olde Good Things
124 West 24th Street
New York, NY 10011
(212) 989-8401
www.oldegoodthings.com
Preservationist salvage, specializing in rare architectural finds.

Salvage One
1840 W. Hubbard
Chicago, IL 60622
(312) 733-0098
www.salvageone.com
American, British, and French architectural artifacts.

United House Wrecking
535 Hope Street
Stamford, CT 06906
(203) 348-5371
www.unitedhousewrecking.com
Architectural antiques, including stained glass, lighting and plumbing fixtures, doors, windows, marble and wood mantels, and ironwork.

Urban Archaeology
143 Franklin Street
New York, NY 10013
(212) 431-4646
www.urbanarchaeology.com
Architectural antiques as well as reproduction bathroom and lighting fixtures.

Barns & Log Homes

Antique Cabins and Barns, Inc.
(888) 941-9553 (office)
(304)365-7619 (fax)
www.countrysettings.com
Hand-hewn log cabins, timber frame barns, hand-hewn beams, barn siding, chestnut lumber, antique oak lumber, and various other vintage building materials.

Bear Creek Lumber
P.O. Box 669
Winthrop, WA 98862
(800) 597-7191
www.bearcreeklumber.com
Hard-to-find woods, such as Western red cedar and Alaskan yellow cedar.

Big Spring Preservation Group, Inc.
101 Tateho Road
Greeneville, TN 37743
(423) 787-9373
www.bigspringpreservation.com
Salvaged log houses, log barns, and outbuildings of all types and styles, as well as post-and-beam frame barns and timber-frame houses.

Cabin & Timber
835 East Pattison Street
Ely, MN 55731
(218) 365-6609
www.cabintimber.com
Purchasing, disassembling, transporting, restoring, and reconstructing antique logs buildings, and timber frame barns.

Duluth Timber Company
P.O. Box 16717
Duluth, MN 55816
(218) 727-2145
www.duluthtimber.com
Reclaimed lumber and timber, beams and millwork from lumber salvaged from old buildings.

Emmert International
11811 S.E. Highway 212
Clackamas, OR 97015
(503) 655-7191
www.emmertintl.com
Structural moving and historical landmark structure relocation. Heavy hauling and house moving.

Log Home Restoration Worldwide LLC
P.O. Box 232
Canaan, NH 03741
(888) FIXLOGS
www.fixlogs.com
Restoration of new and old log, cedar-shingled and cedar-sided homes. Interior and exterior cleaning, sealing, chinking and replacement services.

New Heritage Woodworking
102 Eureka Dr.
Manlius, NY 13104
(315) 682-0220
www.newheritagewoodworking.com
Custom timber frame design and construction.

Ozark Mountain Wood Preservatives
4360 Rixey Road, Suite 4
North Little Rock, AR 72117
(800) 441-1564
www.ozarkmtn.com
Sealants, stains, preservatives, and other log home restoration supplies.

Restoration Resources
P.O. Box 525
Alna, ME 04535
(207) 586-5680
www.oldhouserestoration.com
Historic barn and house inspections, interior and exterior restoration, building services , and research documentation.

Timeless Wood Care Products, Inc.
6526 Schamber Road
Muskegon, MI 49444
(800) 564-2987
www.timelesswoodcare.com
Log home restoration and maintenance care products.

Vermont Frames
P.O. Box 100
Hinesburg, VT 05461
(800) 545-6290
Builder of quality timber and frame structures.

Vintage Barns, Woods & Restorations, Inc.
294 Whiteport Road
Hidden Valley Lake Manor House
Kingston , NY 12401
(845) 340-9870
www.vintagewoods.com
Design consultation, barn reconstruction, barn home conversions, log house restoration, and antique materials.

Carpet, Fabric & Wallpaper

Bradbury & Bradbury Art Wallpapers
P.O. Box 155
Bernicia, CA 94510
(707) 746-1900
www.bradbury.com
Hand-printed Victorian- and Edwardian-style wallpapers.

Brunschwig & Fils
75 Virginia Road
North White Plains, NY 10603
(914) 684-5800
www.brunschwig.com
Reproduction 18th-, 19th-, and 20th-century fabric, trimmings, and wallpapers. To the trade only.

J.R. Burrows & Company
P.O. Box 522
Rockland, MA 02370
(800) 347-1795
www.burrows.com
Reproduction wallpaper, carpets, and fabric, including designs from the English and American Arts & Crafts Movement.

Elizabeth Eakins Cotton
5 Taft Street
Norwalk, CT 06854
(203) 831-9347
hand-dyed handwoven cotton rugs in traditional patterns.

Historic Wallpaper Specialties
267 Watertank Hill Road
Johnson City, TN 37604
(423) 929-8552
www.historicwallpapering.com
Installation and conservation of historic wallpaper world wide.

Specification Chemicals, Inc.
824 Keeler
P.O. Box 709
Boone, IA 50036
(800) 247-3932
(515) 432-8256
www.spec-chem.com
Restoration and reinforcement of plaster walls and ceilings.

Charles Rupert
2005 Oak Bay Avenue
Victoria, BC V8R 1E5
Canada
(250) 592-4916
www.charles-rupert.com
Historic wallpapers, fabrics, tiles, and home accessories.

Sanderson
979 Third Avenue, Suite 409
New York, NY 10022
(212) 319-7220
Fabrics and wallcoverings based on original designs. Exclusive supplier of William Morris-designed wallpapers. To the trade only.

Scalamandré
300 Trade Zone Drive
Ronkonkoma, NY 11779
(800) 932-4361
www.scalamandre.com
Reproduction and restoration fabrics, wallcoverings, and trimmings. To the trade only.

Schumacher
79 Madison Avenue
New York, NY 10016
(800) 988-7775
Decorative textiles for wallpaper, floorcoverings, and trimmings. To the trade only.

Stark Carpet Corporation
979 Third Avenue
New York, NY 10022
(212) 752-9000
www.starkcarpet.com
Custom-designed carpets and fabrics. To the trade only.

Woodard & Greenstein/ Woodard Weave
506 East 74th Street, 5th Floor
New York, NY 10021
(800) 332-7847
www.woodardweave.com
Flat-woven area rugs and runners in traditional American designs.

Clapboards & Millwork

Barnes Lumber Manufacturing, Inc.
Georgia Highway 24 East
Statesboro, GA 30459
(800) 441-2340
www.barneslumber.com
Architectural millwork, custom wood ceilings, clapboards and siding, columns and capitals, wood flooring, mantels, moldings, cornices, and salvaged lumber.

Blue Ox Millworks
1 X Street
Eureka, CA 95501
(800) 248-4259
www.blueoxmill.com
Historically accurate millwork, including moldings, balusters, and handrails.

Chadsworth, Inc.
P.O. Box 53268
Atlanta, GA 30355
(404) 876-5410
www.columns.com
Interior and exterior architectural wooden columns.

Cumberland Woodcraft Co.
P.O. Drawer 609
Carlisle, PA 17013
(800)367-1884
www.cumberlandwoodcraft.com
Wood corbels, brackets, moldings, paneling, lattice, and porch parts.

Donnell's Clapboard Mill
Box 1560
County Road
Sedgwick, ME 04676
(207) 359-2036
Authentic 18th- and 19th-century radial cut and quartersawn pine clapboard in all sizes.

Goodwin Heart Pine Company
106 SW 109 Place
Micanopy, FL 32667
(800) 336-3118
www.heartpine.com
Flooring, trim, paneling, lumber, stair parts, and mantels in standard or custom dimensions from river-recovered heart pine and heart cypress.

Granville Manufacturing Company
Route 100
Granville, VT 05747
(802) 767-4747
www.woodsiding.com
Spruce and pine quartersawn clapboards as well as sidings, trim boards, wood flooring, shakes, and shingles.

Littleton Millwork
44 Lafayette Avenue
Littleton, NH 03561
(603) 444-2677
Custom woodwork for historic restorations, specializing in doors and sash windows.

Mantels of Yesteryear
70 West Tennessee Avenue
McCaysville, GA 30555
(706) 492-5534
www.mantelsofyesteryear.com
Antique and reproduction mantelpieces.

New England Classic, Inc.
3 Adams Street
S. Portland, ME 04106
(888) 880-6324
www.homefittings.com
Traditionally styled, do-it-yourself wood paneling systems. Call for local dealer.

Timeless Timber
2200 East Lake Shore Drive
Ashland, WI 54806
(715) 685-9663
www.timelesstimber.com
Mantels, moldings, flooring, and furniture from old logs recovered from lakes and rivers.

Ward Clapboard
P.O. Box 1030
Waitsfield, VT 05673
(802) 496-3581
Quartersawn pine clapboards; mill uses century-old radial saws to slice logs into six-foot-long boards.

Flooring

Aged Woods, Inc.
2331 East Market Street
York, PA 17402
(800) 233-9307
Antique wood floorboards, ceilings, and wall panels.

Albany Woodworks
P.O. Box 729
Albany, LA 70711
(800) 551-1282
www.albanywoodworks.com
Antique pine flooring, moldings, paneling, and stair treads.

Authentic Pine Floors
4042 Highway 42
Locust Grove, GA 30248
(800) 283-6038
www.authenticpinefloors.com
Kiln-dried Southern yellow pine and heart pine flooring.

Carlisle Wide Plank Floors
1676 Route 9
Stoddard, NH 03464
(800) 595-9663
www.wideplankflooring.com
Wide plank flooring, recycled woods, custom paneling, and stair parts.

Centre Mills Antique Floors
P.O. Box 16
Aspers, PA 17304
(717) 334-0249
www.igateway.com/mall/homeimp/wood/index.htm
Flooring and hand-hewn beams in old and rare wood, including wormy chestnut, rustic oak, heart pine, yellow pine, and early white pine and fir.

Chestnut Specialists, Inc.
(860) 283-4209
Wideboard and plank antique flooring remilled from antique lumber, including a large inventory of chestnut, oak, and pine.

Conklin's Authentic Barnwood & Hand Hewn Beams
RR 1 Box 70
Susquehanna, PA 18847
(570) 465-3832
www.conklinsbarnwood.com
Flooring, barnsiding, and beams from reclaimed barnwood.

Mountain Lumber
P.O. Box 289
Ruckersville, VA 22968
(800) 445-2671
www.mountainlumber.com
Reclaimed and remilled beams, decking, and columns. Longleaf heart pine and other antique wood remilled into hardwood flooring, stair parts, and moldings.

The Old House Parts Company
24 Blue Wave Mall
Kennebunk, ME 04043
(207) 985-1999
www.oldhouseparts.com
Custom construction using antique pine, installation of antique flooring, and old home design services.

Sylvan Brandt, LLC
651 East Main Street
Lititz, PA 17543
(717) 626-4520
www.sylvanbrandt.com
Reclaimed flooring from a variety of woods.

Hardware

Antique Hardware & Home
19 Buckingham Plantation Drive
Bluffton, SC 29910
(800) 422-9982
www.antiquehardware.com
Clawfoot bathtubs, shower conversions, faucets, sinks, and high-tank toilets.

Baldwin Hardware Corporation
841 East Wyomissing Boulevard
Box 15048
Reading, PA 19612
(800) 566-1986
Brass hardware reproductions. Call for dealer locations.

Ball and Ball Antique Hardware Reproductions
463 West Lincoln Highway
Exton, PA 19341
(800) 257-3711
www.ballandball.com
Reproduction hardware.

Brandywine Valley Forge
P.O. Box 1129
Valley Forge, PA 19482
(610) 948-9629
www.bvforge.com
Hand-forged shutter, gate, and barn hardware.

Ed Donaldson Hardware Restorations
1488 York Road
Carlisle, PA 17013
(717) 249-3624
www.eddonaldson.com
Antique and reproduction hardware including doorknobs, doorbells, knockers, locks, and hinges.

Liz's Antique Hardware
453 South La Brea
Los Angeles, CA 90036
(323) 939-4403
www.lahardware.com
*Period hardware for doors, windows, and lighting,
as well as reproduction hardware and lighting.*

**Monroe Coldren & Son Antique 18th
and 19th Century Hardware**
723 E. Virginia Avenue
West Chester, PA 19380
(610) 692-5651
www.monroecoldren.com
Antique hardware and custom reproductions.

Restoration Hardware
(800) 762-1005
www.restorationhardware.com
*Traditional cabinet hardware, furniture, light-
ing, and quirky household items. Call for store
locations.*

Tremont Nail Company
P.O. Box 111
Wareham, MA 02571
(800) 842-0560
www.tremontnail.com
Historically accurate nails.

Lighting

American Period Lighting
3004 Columbia Avenue
Lancaster, PA 17603
(717) 392-5649
www.americanperiod.com
*Reproductions of 18th-century indoor and out-
door lighting.*

Authentic Designs
69 The Mill Road
West Rupert, VT 05776
(802) 394-7713
www.authentic-designs.com
*Reproduction Early American and Colonial
lighting fixtures.*

Brass Reproductions Lighting
9711 Canoga Avenue
Chatsworth, CA 91311
(800) 828-5858
www.brassrepro.com
*Brass reproduction Victorian and traditional
lighting.*

Gaslight Time
5 Plaza Street West
Brooklyn, NY 11217
(718) 789-7185
*Restored Victorian and period lighting, from the
1850s to the 1930s.*

Lighting by Hammerworks
118 Main Street
Meredith, NH 11217
(603) 279-7352
www.hammerworks.com
*Reproduction interior and exterior lighting fix-
tures made in copper, brass, and tin. Also hand-
forged door and shutter hardware.*

C. Neri Antiques & Lighting
315 South Street
Philadelphia, PA 19147
(215) 923-6669
www.neriantiquelighting.com
Antique lighting fixtures.

Period Lighting Fixtures
(800) 828-6990
*Handmade reproduction lighting from the 18th
and 19th centuries.*

Rejuvenation
2550 NW Nicolai Street
Portland, OR 97210
(888) 401-1900
www.rejuvenation.com
*Brass reproduction interior and exterior lighting
in a variety of historic styles.*

St. Louis Antique Lighting Co.
801 North Sinker Boulevard
St. Louis, MO 63130
(314) 863-1414
*Antique handcrafted brass reproduction ceiling
fixtures, sconces, and lamps. Gas, electric, and
combination fixtures from 1880 to 1930.*

Victorian Revival
1150 Castlefield Avenue
Toronto, ON M6B 1E9
(416) 789-1704
www.victorian-revival.com
*Antique and vintage lighting, specializing in
Victorian-period items.*

Moldings & Trim

Arvid's Historic Woods
19420 21st Avenue West
Linwood, WA 98036
(800) 627-8437
*Molding profiles ranging in style from historic
reproductions to custom-designed contemporary.*

Focal Point
300 Anaconda Drive
Tarboro, NC 27886
(800) 662-5550
www.focalpointap.com
*Moldings, medallions, domes, and other architec-
tural ornaments. Carries the Frank Lloyd Wright,
Williamsburg, and other historic lines.*

Haas Wood & Ivory Works
184A Harbor Way
South San Francisco, CA 94080
(650) 588-1082
*Ornamental details, including drawer pulls,
porhc columns, and arched and curved moldings.*

**Hyde Park Fine Art Of Mouldings,
Inc.**
29-16 40th Avenue
Long Island City, NY 11101
(718) 706-0504
www.hyde-park.com
*Plaster reproductions of ornamental details using
centuries-old plaster techniques—including capitals, ceiling medallions, and crown moldings.*

Mad River Woodworks
P.O. Box 1067
Blue Lake, CA 95525
(707) 668-5671
www.madriverwoodworks.com
Wood moldings, paneling, and porch aprts.

San Francisco Victoriana
2070 Newcomb Avenue
San Francisco, CA 94124
(415) 648-0313
*Decorative moldings, ornamental plaster an
wood, rosette ceilings, brackets, cornices, and
medallions.*

J.P. Weaver
941 Air Way
Glendale, CA 91201
(818) 500-1740
*Clay-based reproductions of detailed architectur-
al elements.*

Paints

Benjamin Moore & Company
51 Chestnut Ridge Road
Montvale, NJ 07645
(800) 344-0400
www.benjaminmoore.com
*Interior/exterior historical color collection,
grouped by historic style. Call for dealer locations.*

Christopher Norman, Inc.
41 West 25th Street, Tenth Floor
New York, NY 10010
(212) 647-0303
www.christophernorman.com
*Experts in historic paints and the American dis-
tributor of UK-based Farrow & Ball paints. Call
for dealer locations.*

Glidden
(800) GLIDDEN
www.gliddenpaint.com
Interior and exterior paints. Call for dealer locations.

Martin-Senour Paints
(800) MSP-5270
www.martinsenour.com
Williamsburg historic color collection. Call for dealer locations.

MB Historic Décor
P.O. Box 1255
Quechee, VT 05059
(888) 649-1790
www.mbhistoricdecor.com
Historically accurate New England-style wall and floor stencils.

The Old Fashioned Milk Paint Co., Inc.
436 Main Street
Groton, MA 01450
(866) 350-6455
www.milkpaint.com
Genuine milk paint in a variety of colors. Call for dealer locations.

Old Village Paint
P.O. Box 1030
Fort Washington, PA 19034
(610) 238-9001
www.old-village.com
Colonial, Federal, and Victorian period colors.

Alex Pifer's Seraph
420 Main Street
Sturbridge, MA 01566
(508) 347-2241
www.theseraph.com
Paint and stencils, as well as authentic textiles, blacksmith items, and lighting.

The Sherwin-Williams Company
(800) 4-SHERWIN
www.sherman-williams.com
Interior and exterior paint. Call for dealer locations.

Valspar Paint
(888) 350-3703
www.valspar.com
Historic color collections. Free color matching services through "The Color Doctor." Call for dealer locations.

Plumbing

A-Ball Plumbing Supply
1703 West Burnside Street
Portland, OR 97209
(800) 228-0134
www.a-ball.com
Vintage plumbing restoration.

American Standard
P.O. Box 6820
1 Centennial Plaza
Piscataway, NJ 08855
(800) 442-1902
www.americanstandard-us.com
Plumbing, fixtures, and faucets, including the Reminiscence Collection, which was inspired by vintage styles.

Barclay Products
4000 Porette Drive
Gurnee, IL 60031
(847) 244-1234
Plumbing products, including clawfoot tubs and pedestal sinks. Call for local dealer.

Baths from the Past Collection
83 East Water Street
Rockland, MA 02371
(800) 697-3971
www.faucetfactory.com
Reproduction Victorian, Edwardian, and traditional faucets, shower systems, and pedestal sinks as well as custom plumbing for classic bathrooms.

Kohler Plumbing
444 Highland Drive
Kohler, WI 53044
(800) 4-KOHLER
www.kohlerco.com
Bathroom and kitchen faucets and fixtures. Call for local dealers.

Mac the Antique Plumber
6325 Elvas Avenue
Sacramento, CA 95819
(800) 916-BATH
www.antiqueplumber.com
Antique plumbing supplies, including leg-tub shower enclosures, high- and low-tank toilets, sinks, and a variety of bathroom accessories.

Restoration Works
P.O. Box 486
Buffalo, NY 14205
(716) 913-2522
www.restoworks.com
Decorative hardware, plumbing fixtures, and accessories, architectural trim, columns, tin ceilings, ceiling medallions, and lighting.

Waterworks
29 Park Avenue
Danbury, CT 06810
(800) 899-6757
Reproduction kitchen and bathroom fixtures and fitting in Edwardian and Bell-Epoque styles.

Stone, Brick & Metalwork

Architectural Iron Company
P.O. Box 126
Milford, PA 18337
(570) 296-7722
www.archiron.com
Manufacture and restoration of wrought- and cast-iron fences.

Boral Bricks
(800) 5-BORAL-5
www.boralbricks.com
Individually crafted 17th-century brick reproductions. Call for dealer locations.

Moultrie Manufacturing Company
1403 Georgia Highway 133 South
Moultrie, GA 31768
(800) 841-8674
www.moultriemanufacturing.com
Metal gates, fences, columns, and railings.

W.F. Norman Corp.
214 North Cedar Street
Nevada, MO 63772
(800) 641-4038
Steel ceilings, moldings, ornaments, weathervanes, and finials.

Sheldon Slate Products Company
Fox Road
Middle Granville, NY 12849
(518) 642-9085
www.sheldonslate.com
Slate floor tile, flagging, structural slate and roofing, monuments, and slate sinks.

The Stewart Iron Works Company
P.O. Box 2612
20 West 18th Street
Covington, KY 41012
(859) 431-1985
www.stewartironworks.com
Historic ironwork.

Summitville Tiles, Inc.
(330) 223-1511
www.summitville.com
Tile and brick, including the historic Williamsburg Tile Collection.

Vermont Soapstone Co.
P.O. Box 268
248 Stoughton Pond Road
Perkinsville, VT 05151
(802) 263-5404
www.vermontsoapstone.com
Soapstone sinks, counter, and fireplaces.

Wind & Weather
1200 North Main Street
Fort Bragg, CA 95437
(800) 922-9463
www.windandweather.com
Weather vanes, sundials, weather instruments, and cupolas.

Woodbury Blacksmith & Forge CO.
125 Main Street South
Woodbury, CT 06798
(203) 263-5737
Reproduction 17th- and 18th-century hardware and accessories produced using original methods.

Windows & Doors

Andersen Corporation
100 Fourth Avenue North
Bayport, MN 55003
(651) 264-5150
www.andersoncorp.com
Windows and doors in a variety of sizes, shapes, and styles. Call for local dealers.

Architectural Components, Inc.
26 North Leverett Road
Montague, MA 01351
(413) 367-9441
Reproduction and custom wood windows and doors.

Bendheim
61 Willett Street
Passaic, NJ 07055
(800) 835-5304
www.bendheim.com
Restoration glass made using original cylinder method.

J.S. Benson Woodworking & Design
118 Birge Street
Brattleboro, VT 05301
(800) 339-3515
Custom-designed and historically accurate doors, windows, and accessories; custom door and window hardware.

Blaine Window Hardware, Inc.
17319 Blaine Drive
Hagerstown, MD 21740
(800) 678-1919
www.blainewindow.com
Replacement hardware for windows and doors.

Blenko Glass Company, Inc.
P.O. Box 67
Milton, WV 25541
(304) 734-9081
www.blenkoglass.com
Hand-blown reproduction glass.

Doors of London
9705 Mill Station Road
Sebastopol, CA 95472
(707) 887-1879
www.doorsoflondon.com
Antique doors and an assortment of English architectural antiques.

Hunter Douglas
(888) HDVIEWS
www.hunterdouglas.com
Traditional window shades. Call for dealer locations.

Jennifer's Glassworks, Inc.
4875 South Atlanta Road
Atlanta, GA 30080
(800) 241-3388
www.jennifersglassworks.com
Leaded, beveled, and stained glass windows and doors.

Kestrel Shutters
9 East Race Street
Stowe, PA 19464
(800) 494-4321
www.diyshutters.com
Cedar and basswood shutters and folding screen styles for historic renovation.

Lamson-Taylor Custom Doors & Millwork
191 Tucker Road
South Acworth, NH 03607
(603) 835-2992
www.lamsontaylor.com
Custom doors manufactured from native New England woods.

Marvin Windows and Doors
P.O. Box 100
Warroad, MN 56763
(888) 537-7828
www.marvin.com
Custom windows, Call for dealer locations.

Nostalgic Warehouse, Inc.
4661 Monaco Street
Denver, CO 80216
(972) 271-0319
Custom manufactured reproduction door and cabinet hardware using traditional patterns. Call for dealer locations.

Pella Corporation
102 Main Street
Pella, Iowa 50219
(800) 374-4758
www.pella.com
Windows and doors. Call for dealer locations.

Shuttercraft, Inc.
282 Stepstone Hill Road
Guilford, CT 06437
(203) 245-2608
www.shuttercraftinc.com
Traditionally styled shutters.

The Shutter Depot
437 LaGrange Street
Greenville, GA 30222
(706) 672-1214
www.shutterdepot.com
Plantation-style moveable louver shutters.

Southern Heritage Shutters
5690 Summer Avenue
Memphis, TN 38134
(901) 751-1000
www.quantumselect.com
Traditionally styled interior and exterior shutters.

Timberlane Woodcrafters, Inc.
197 Wissahickon Avenue
North Wales, PA 19454
(800) 250-2221
www.timberlane-wood.com
Traditional exterior wood shutters.

Weather Shield Windows & Doors
One Weather Shield Plaza.
P.O. Box 309
Medford, WI 54451
(800) 477-6808
www.weathershield.com
Traditionally styled windows and doors. Call for dealer locations.

Canada Associations

Canadian Conservation Institute
1030 Innes Road
Ottawa ON K1A 0M5
Canada
(613) 998-3721
http://www.cci-icc.gc.ca/

Canadian Heritage Information Network
15 Eddy Street, (15-4-A)
Gatineau, Quebec
Canada K1A 0M5
(819) 994-1200
www.chin.gc.ca

The Association of Registered Interior Designers of Ontario
717 Church Street
Toronto, ON
M4W 2M5
(416) 921-2127
www.arido.on.ca

Suppliers

Americana Log Homes
29 chemin Cousineau
L'Ange-Gardien, QC
J8L 2W7, Canada
(819) 986-9282
Barns & Log Homes

**Carpet Canada
GoPro Canada Inc.**
2510 Yonge St. Suite 205
Toronto, Ontario
Canada
M4P 2H
(416) 385-2433
www.carpet.ca

Farrow & Ball (Canada)
1054 Yonge Street
Toronto
Ontario
T (416) 920 0200
http://www.farrow-ball.com/
Paint

Flooring Giant
Flooring Giant Head Office
23 Kodiak Cres
North York, Ontario
M3J 3E5
(800) 268-5132
www.giantcarpet.com
Flooring

High Country Studio
P.O. Box 2894
Invermere, B.C.
V0A 1K0, Canada
250.342.3865
www.highcountrystudio.com
Architectural Salvage

Para Paints
11 Kenview Boulevard
Brampton, Ontario
L6T 5G5
Tel: (905) 792-0940
http://www.para.com/main.html
Paint

Revy Home & Garden Warehouse
www.revy.ca
Hardware

Rona
(866) 283-2239
www.rona.ca
Hardware

Traders of the Lost Ark
5915-1A Street SW T2H 0G4
Calgary, Alberta, CANADA
(403)229-0234
http://www.traderstoo.com/
Architectural Salvage

Australia Associations

Australian Conservation Foundation
Floor 1, 60 Leicester St, Carlton, Vic 3053
(03) 9345 1111
http://www.acfonline.org.au

Australian Government Department of the Environment and Heritage
John Gorton Building
King Edward Terrace
Parkes ACT 2600
GPO Box 787
Canberra ACT 2601
+61 2 6274 1111
http://www.deh.gov.au

Australian Heritage Commission
GPO Box 787
Canberra ACT 2601 AUSTRALIA
Phone: 61 (02) 6274-2111 Fax: 61 (02) 6274-2095
http://www.ahc.gov.au/

**Australia International Council on Monuments and Sites
Cultural Heritage Center for Asia and the Pacific
Faculty of Arts**
Deakin University
Burwood VIC 3125 Australia
+61 3 9251 7131
www.icomos.org/australia/

National Parks & Protected Area Management Committee
Director of National Parks
Parks Australia
Environment Australia
GPO Box 787
CANBERRA ACT 2601
(02) 6274 2220
http://www.deh.gov.au/parks/best-practice/index.html

The Royal Australian Institute of Architects
2a Mugga Way
Red Hill ACT 2603
PO Box 3373
MANUKA ACT 2603
Phone (02) 6273 1548
www.architecture.com.au

Suppliers

Appalachian Log Homes
3A Great Western Highway
Blaxland, NSW
(61) 247395888
www.appalachianloghomes.com.au

Bunnings Warehouse
www.bunnings.com
Hardware

Dulux Paint
www.dulux.com.au
Paint

Great Bear Log Homes
P.O. Box 515
Victoria, Mansfield 3724 Australia
(01161) 35779-1524
www.greatbearloghomes.com.au

Mitre 10
http://www.mitre10.com.au
Hardware

Steptoe's Renovation Supplies
112 Rokeby Street
Collingwood Vic. 3066
03 9419 9366
www.steptoes.com.au
Architectural Salvage

Triton Manufacturing & Design Co. Pty. Ltd.
14-18 Mills Street
Cheltenham, Vic. 3192
1300 655 686
www.triton.net.au
Clapboards & Millwork

The Paint Spot
www.paintspot.com.au
Paint

Index

Designer Credits

Page 17 top
David Drummond
Lititz, PA

Page 19 top
David Graham Architects
Ossining, NY

Pages 26-28
J. Carson Looney
Looney Ricks Kiss Architects
Memphis, TN

Pages 30-33
Woodard and Greenstein
Barn Homes
New York, NY

Kathleen M. Bartlett Designs
Bridgehampton, NY

Pages 34-5
Burr & McCallum Architects
Williamstown, MA

Nicholas Olhy Architect
New Haven, CT

Pages 50-2
Jim McChesney Architect
New York, NY

Cramer and Co. Interior Design
New Rochelle, NY

Page 53 bottom
The Weather Hill Restoration Co.
Charlotte, VT

Jefferey Barnes Architect
and Assoc., Inc.
Manchester, VT

Pages 60-3
Morrie Breyer Interiors
Point Pleasant, PA

Pages 66-69
Donald Kaufman Color
New York, NY

Page 71
Larry Bogdanow & Assoc.,
Architects
New York, NY

Page 73 bottom
Laura Bohn Design Associates,
Inc.
New York, NY

Pages 74-9
Stanley Hura Designs, Inc.
New York, NY

Stuart Silk Architects
Seattle, WA

Pages 85
Stanley Hura Designs, Inc.
New York, NY

Page 93
The New Jersey Barn Co.
Princeton, NJ

Pages 104-5
Stanley Hura Designs, Inc.

Page 110 left, 115
Patricia O'Shaughnessy
New York, NY

Page 116
Wolfman-Gold & Good Co.
New York, NY

Page 128
Maggie McManus
Architectural Interiors
Nyack, NY

Page 144
The Weather Hill Restoration Co.

Pages 154-157
Scot P. Samuelson
Lyme, CT

Page 158 top
J Whitney Huber
Essex, CT

Page 164
The Weather Hill Restoration Co.
Charlotte, VT

Page 166
Woodard and Greenstein
Barn Homes
New York, NY

Photography Credits

Paul Kopelow:
Pages 16, 24, 111, 164, 167.

Steven Mays:
Pages 2, 5, 34 both, 35, 102, 146 bottom, 149 bottom.

Keith Scott Morton:
Pages 1, 6-7, 9, 10, 11, 12, 13, 14, 17, 19 top, 21, 22, 23, 24, 25, 26, 27, 28, 30, 31, 32, 33, 40, 41 both, 42 both, 43, 44, 45, 46-7, 48, 49 both, 50, 51, 52, 53 both, 54, 55, 56-7, 58, 59 top, 65 top, 70, 71, 72, 73 top, 74, 76-7, 78 both, 79, 80-1, 81, 82, 83, 85 both, 86, 86-7, 88, 89, 90, 91, 92, 93, 94, 95, 96-7, 99, 100-1, 103, 104-5, 107, 108-9, 110 both, 113, 114 bottom, 115, 116, 117, 120, 121, 122, 123, 124, 126-7, 130, 131, 132, 133, 135 both, 140, 141, 142-3, 144, 145 both, 147, 148 both, 153 both, 154-5, 156, 157, 158 bottom, 160, 161, 162 both, 163, 165 both, 166 top center, 166 bottom left, 168.

Pizzi/Thompson Associates:
Pages 18 bottom, 65 bottom.

David Prince:
Pages 16, 66, 67, 68, 69 both, 112, 114 top, 119, 134, 137, 138, 139.

Steven Randazzo:
Page 128

William P. Steele:
Pages 15, 17, 60, 61, 62-3, 73 bottom, 129, 158 top, 166 top right.

Jessie Walker:
Pages 18 top, 19 bottom, 29, 37, 38-9, 40, 59 bottom, 64, 84, 118, 146 top, 149 top, 151, 152, 159.